Contents

YORK NOTES

General Editors: Professor A.N. Jeffares (*University of Stirling*) & Professor Suheil Bushrui (*American University of Beirut*)

Margaret Atwood

CAT'S EYE

Notes by Bruce Stewart

MA, PH D (DUBLIN)
Lecturer at the University of Ulster

LONGMAN
YORK PRESS

YORK PRESS
Immeuble Esseily, Place Riad Solh, Beirut

ADDISON WESLEY LONGMAN
Edinburgh Gate, Harlow,
Essex CM20 2JE, United Kingdom
Associated companies, branches and representatives
throughout the world

First published 1996

ISBN 0–582–29350–2

Phototypeset by Gem Graphics, Trenance, Mawgan Porth, Cornwall
Printed in Singapore

Part 1

Introduction

The author

Margaret Eleanor Atwood was born in Ottawa, Ontario, on 18 November 1939. The second of three children, she spent her first years living in the forests of Northern Ontario and Quebec where her father was carrying out field research up to 1946, when he took up a teaching post at the University of Toronto. Having read widely during childhood she decided to become a writer at the age of sixteen, by which time she had already produced some poems, plays and stories. Her early education was conducted at home by her mother; later she attended Leaside High School in Toronto (1952–7) and went on to Victoria College, University of Toronto (1957), graduating in English Literature (1961). Among her teachers there were Northrop Frye, a distinguished Canadian practitioner of archetypal readings of literature, and Jay MacPherson, a writer best known for her retellings of ancient myths for children.

Atwood proceeded to Radcliffe College, Harvard, on a Woodrow Wilson scholarship and completed a master's degree in Victorian literature in 1962, after which she started working on a doctorate on English Gothic fiction. In 1963 she took a job in marketing, and subsequently taught English to engineering students at the University of British Columbia in Vancouver during 1964–5 before finishing her thesis in 1967. She married James Polk in 1967 and divorced him six years later, moving to a farm near Alliston, Ontario, with the novelist Graeme Gibson. In 1980 they settled in Toronto with their daughter Jess. Atwood has also lived and worked in Alabama, Australia, Berlin, Edinburgh, New York, London, French Provence, Texas and Ireland, holding the position of writer-in-residence at universities in several of those places.

Margaret Atwood is widely regarded as Canada's leading contemporary poet and novelist. She has produced a dozen books of poetry between *The Circle Game* (1966) and *Morning in the Burned House* (1995). There are eight Atwood novels and books of short fiction dealing with psychological, cultural and political problems in contemporary Western society with a strong focus on women's issues. In her first novel, *Edible Woman* (1969), the narrator, Marian McAlpin, overcomes a mental illness by baking a cake for her husband to eat instead of eating her. In *Surfacing* (1972) an unnamed female narrator goes searching in the Canadian forests for her lost father, a biologist. *Lady Oracle* (1976) is the story of a woman novelist who has to kill off her literary identities in order to be reborn. In

Bodily Harm (1978) Rennie Wilford, a journalist, flees to the Caribbean to reconstruct her life, and encounters harsh realities there that force her to confront the narcissism of Western culture. *The Handmaid's Tale* (1985), a science-fiction story inspired by right-wing movements in North America, examines a society in the non-too-distant future where women have been turned into slaves. There are five books of short fiction as well, from *Dancing Girls* (1977) to *Good Bones* (1991). Margaret Atwood has also written extensively on Canadian history and literature. *Second Words* (1982) is a selection of her critical prose.

Among more than fifty other awards she has won the Governor's Award on two occasions (1966 and 1986), the Los Angeles Times Prize for Fiction, and most recently the Swedish Humour Association's International Award for *The Robber Bride* in 1995. She has been short-listed twice for the Booker Award. She has been awarded honorary degrees by several Canadian, American, and British universities. Besides her major collections she has published numerous art press collections of poetry including her first pamphlet, *Double Persephone* (which won the E. J. Pratt Medal in 1961), and has written for radio and television. She has also made recordings for Caedmon (poetry) and American Audio Prose. Audio-cassettes of her novels are available.

President of the Writers' Union of Canada (1981–2), she lectures regularly on Canadian literature around the world. In 1984–6 she served as President of PEN. A consistent opponent of social injustice, she has worked with Amnesty International. While editor at the House of Anansi Press in Toronto (1971–3), she nurtured opportunities for women writers and has continued to do so.

The novel

The plot of *Cat's Eye* contains some obvious resemblances to the early life of its author, who – like Elaine Risley – was brought up in the wilds of Northern Ontario while her father was engaged in entomological research. It is the most obviously (and perhaps deceptively) autobiographical of her books, in all of which she uses the first-person form of writing. In an address to the American Booksellers Association in June 1993 she said:

> I spent much of my early life in a forest. I don't mean a village in a forest. I mean a forest, pure and simple ... This sounds like an idyllic childhood, and in a way it was. But in addition to no electricity and no running water, there were also no movies, no theatres, no art galleries, and no radios on which you could get much more than a crackling noise during thunderstorms. There were however many books ... I was traumatised early in life by the death of that poor horse in Orwell's *Animal Farm*, which I thought was going to be about user-friendly

bunnies, sort of like Peter Rabbit; and I became haunted by the accusing voyeuristic eye-in-the-keyhole that used to be on the covers of the Dell murder mysteries.

The 'trauma' of the author's childhood mentioned here is very different from that which affects Elaine Risley. The time that Elaine spends at Queen Mary Public School has no equivalent in the real 'autobiography' of the writer, offering no corresponding episodes of bullying. The fact that the narrator is a painter should not be overlooked either. In a prefatory note to *Cat's Eye* Margaret Atwood insists on the fictional basis of both plot and characters, adding this as well: 'The opinions expressed are those of the characters and should not be confused with the author's.' At other times she has spoken of her increasing annoyance at the 'autobiographical constructions' imposed upon her novels, along with 'all those autobiographical questions' she often faces at lectures and readings.

Undoubtedly, however, there are passages in *Cat's Eye* that seem to echo the opinions of the author. One of the delights of the book consists in just those condensed essays on a range of topics relating to the present state of Western culture that form in Elaine Risley's mind as she narrates the story. Prominent among them are the amusing potted histories of Western art in Chapters 51 and 58, or the salutary reflections on the way death is treated in Mexican and North American art:

In Mexico they do this festival [All Souls' Eve] the right way . . . Bright candy skulls, family picnics on the graves . . . Everyone goes away happy, including the dead. We've rejected that easy flow between dimensions: we want the dead unmentionable, we refuse to name them, we refuse to feed them. Our dead as a result are thinner, greyer, harder to hear, and hungrier (p. 387).

In another part of the novel the narrator reflects how her attitudes to political leaders have changed now that they are her own age (and Atwood's also, as it happens). In an eloquent passage, she recalls her naïve faith in them when she was younger and admits to wondering now what greed, what furies drive them on (p. 265). Are such opinions merely ascribable to Elaine Risley as narrator of the story, or do they belong to the author in spite of her blanket denial? How is a line to be drawn between fictional autobiography and autobiographical fiction? Such questions mark out *Cat's Eye* as a post-modernist novel. It is also, of course, an example of acute responsiveness to the uncertainties of the world in which we live, and each reader has ultimately to make sense of the novel – just as it is up to him or her to make sense of this world.

Cat's Eye was first published by McClelland and Stewart of Toronto in 1988. Pages cited in these notes refer to the Virago Press edition of 1990, which has been reprinted several times.

Part 2

Summaries
of CAT'S EYE

A general summary

Cat's Eye reconstructs a traumatic experience in the childhood of a painter called Elaine Risley. Through her dreams and paintings she gradually recovers repressed memories of the psychological torment inflicted on her by her school-friend Cordelia. The final stage in her recovery is triggered by a cat's eye marble that served Elaine as a sort of talisman protecting her against a complete loss of identity while she was in Cordelia's power. Years later Elaine finds the marble among her childhood possessions in her mother's house. With that the whole series of events surrounding her traumatised childhood returns to her consciousness. Then she can begin the healing process and, ultimately, the process of forgiving Cordelia.

The novel takes the form of a present-tense narrative set in contemporary Toronto. In the course of this are related a series of autobiographical events set in an earlier period in the same city. In the contemporary parts of the narrative Risley, who has returned there for a retrospective exhibition after twenty years' absence, reflects on changes in the city, compared with the Toronto of her childhood. Her visits to the gallery provide occasions for reflection on the fashionable art world and the people who inhabit it. She also meets her ex-husband Jon, first for lunch, next for dinner; and then they sleep together 'for the comfort of it'.

As the opening of the exhibition approaches, Risley anticipates the arrival of Cordelia at the gallery with increasing apprehension. She feels that she and Cordelia are now twins, linked by the terrible experience of her childhood: Elaine needs to know from Cordelia 'why' it happened, and Cordelia needs Elaine's reflection of the 'part of herself' that had such a damaging impact on Elaine in their schooldays. In the event Cordelia does not arrive: presumably her mental health, shaky when Elaine last encountered her, has continued to deteriorate. Revisiting the scenes of childhood on the morning following the opening, Elaine Risley extends a gesture of forgiveness towards the girl who victimised her, and who is now herself a victim of the dysfunctional relationship with her (Cordelia's) father that caused her to act so destructively towards the narrator.

The retrospective sections, the largest part of the novel, start in early childhood when Elaine travels with her family throughout Northern Ontario, where her father is doing field research on forest insects. Her brother Stephen is her only companion. Her mother teaches them until the family settles when her father takes a post in the University of Toronto. They live in a barely finished house in Toronto's new suburbs, the children attending Queen Mary Public School, where Elaine meets other girls for the first time. Carol Campbell and Grace Smeath become her friends. After the summer holidays they are joined by a third girl, Cordelia.

Cordelia is more sophisticated than the others: her family is better off; her elder sisters, Perdie and Mirrie, already teenagers, are said to be gifted; her home is decorated more fashionably; she is less provincial. It later emerges, however, that she is constantly in trouble with her father, who does not seem to like her. Probably in response to this Cordelia starts bullying Elaine, who has no defence against such an onslaught. Cordelia digs a hole in the garden and, with the other girls, puts Elaine inside it before covering her with boards and earth. This is the moment at which Elaine 'loses power' to Cordelia.

Elaine remembers nothing accurately about this burial but it transforms her inner life completely. Cordelia continues to abuse her while pretending it is for her own good, and Elaine is unable to free herself. She is 'enthralled'; she cannot tell on Cordelia because she is bound by a childish belief in loyalty, and, besides, is afraid that she will lose her friends if she does so. She becomes introverted and self-destructive, peeling off the skin on her feet and biting her nails. It is a period of tense depression; both her appearance and her schoolwork suffer. In the following year, Cordelia's bullying becomes even more relentless. Elaine hears a voice inside her head encouraging her to jump off the bridge that they cross daily on the way from school. She recognises it as Cordelia's: if she jumps, it seems to say, Cordelia will be pleased with her. On Valentine's Day Elaine learns something important when she gets more cards than the other girls: boys are her allies. She keeps it secret.

Cordelia continues to invent ingenious ways of tormenting Elaine, making her stand outside the door for long periods in punishment for imaginary failings. She also manages to erode the relationship between Elaine and her father, tricking Elaine into calling him a 'bugger' (because, as an entomologist, he catches 'bugs'). Elaine learns that she can faint to get out of places that she does not want to be in, and she refines this, developing the trick of seeming to stand aside from her body even without fainting. She has become attached to a marble with a blue centre of the kind known by the children as a 'cat's eye'. This eye can 'see' things without feeling anything, and Elaine cultivates the belief that she can see in a similar way. It is her talisman and her only protection against Cordelia, especially since her mother does not understand the nature of her victimisation and is completely unable to help her. The Risley parents think that Cordelia has beautiful manners and assume her to be their daughter's 'best friend'.

Grace Smeath's mother is an evangelical Protestant and Elaine is taken to church on Sundays with the family. The Smeaths instil in her a form of religious piety. Guilt associated with it is reinforced by blame for belonging to a non-practising family. One day she overhears Mrs Smeath speaking of her as a 'heathen'; the unfairness of it fills Elaine with pure hatred for Mrs Smeath, who evidently knows about the bullying that she is undergoing at the hands of the other girls but regards it as God's punishment for the atheism of her parents. Elaine turns for comfort to a holy picture of the Blessed Virgin which she has found on the road. She kneels and prays to the heart of Mary which is shown on the outside of her chest in the picture. The glowing heart that she imagines she can see in answer to her prayers looks like a red purse that she received as a Christmas present in her first year in Toronto.

In the spring of Elaine's tenth year Cordelia's bullying reaches its climax when she sends her down into the ravine beneath the bridge to fetch her hat which Cordelia has thrown there as a punishment. Elaine falls through the ice of the creek and begins to freeze. When she reaches the bank she 'sees' a 'lady' on the bridge above her: it is the Blessed Virgin, who tells her she can go home. Elaine's mother, told by the girls that she has stayed at school, goes out looking for her and finds her on the road. She is put to bed and the girls are made to apologise. When next they meet, Cordelia accuses her of telling on them, but Elaine (who has actually revealed nothing) finds the strength to say that she does not care what they think. Through this gesture of self-assertion she is suddenly liberated from Cordelia and the others, and she quickly grows apart from them.

Cordelia now moves upwards to another class and then is moved to another school because she is doing badly. When Elaine moves to high school Cordelia's mother contacts hers and the two girls meet again. Elaine remembers nothing of her earlier experiences, and they spend their years together in high school as best friends. They date boys together, but Cordelia is no good at this; her intense manner frightens them. She fails school tests in spite of Elaine's coaching, and it is clear she will not go to university. One day Cordelia talks about the holes she used to dig in her garden. Elaine reacts by ceasing to see Cordelia, though without realising why. Soon she leaves high school for the university, where she studies art and archaeology instead of biology, her best subject, as her father would have liked, being a biologist himself. She also attends night classes at the Toronto College of Art, having decided to be a painter.

At the Art School her life-drawing teacher, Mr Hrbik (a Hungarian), who has seduced a fellow student, Susie, now seduces Elaine at a moment when she is ready to give up her virginity. She is now a drinking companion of some of the male students. One of them, Jon, takes her back to his flat where they make love. In the ensuing months, she continues seeing both Hrbik and Jon. Susie becomes pregnant and haemorrhages during a home abortion, and Elaine, who finds her, soon rejects Hrbik whose self-commiseration have come to seem oppressive to her. She lives with Jon and, when she herself becomes pregnant, they marry. She has a daughter, Sarah.

Sometime earlier, she had begun to paint with egg tempera; now she is painting objects recalled from her childhood in this medium. With three other members of a women's group she holds a joint exhibition that enjoys a *succès de scandale*. Nevertheless, her confidence is steadily eroded by Jon, who regards her work as irrelevant and wants her to stop painting. He considers marriage 'bourgeois' and has relationships with other women. Elaine visits Cordelia in a private mental hospital where she has been placed after a suicide attempt. When Elaine refuses to shelter her, Cordelia accuses her of having always hated her, but Elaine cannot remember ever having felt that way about her. Later, in a moment of depression, Elaine hears Cordelia's childhood voice encouraging her to commit suicide and she cuts her wrist. Jon brings her to hospital but, frightened that she might succeed another time, she decides to leave Toronto, which seems to have such a depressing effect on her.

Taking Sarah with her, Elaine travels to Vancouver, where she establishes herself as a painter. She briefly attends a psychiatrist, but finds a cure for her depressions through her painting, which increasingly reflects the traumas of her childhood. At this stage, she does not yet grasp the significance of her Mrs Smeath series (*Empire Bloomers*) and other paintings based on her still-repressed memories of two lost years. She meets a travel agent called Ben who is much more ordinary than she is, but provides her with stability and love. After a vacation in Mexico they get married. Elaine has another daughter. Her paintings begin to command good prices. Her brother Stephen, who has become a brilliant astrophysicist, is killed by Arab terrorists on board a plane on his way to Frankfurt. Her parents, who have moved north again, never recover from his death. Her father dies suddenly; her mother contracts a lingering disease.

One day while sorting family mementoes with her in the cellar, Elaine comes across the cat's eye marble where she put it away inside the red purse. The sight of it causes her lost memories of childhood to return to her. These memories supply much of the material for her further paintings, including *Cat's Eye*, a self-portrait of sorts with three girls in the background.

After the 'retrospective', Risley revisits the bridge where she nearly died, and later flies back to Vancouver. She has made her peace with Cordelia in a fashion. On the plane she expresses regrets not for the things that happened but for the things that will never happen: two old ladies enjoying old age together.

Detailed summaries

I: Iron Lung

No painting of this name is described in the novel but it is likely that Risley has produced one because she has had a dream on this subject (p. 250).

Chapter 1
A short opening section states the theory of time that Risley's brother Stephen once taught her. His hyper-modern notion of the universe as a space–time continuum supports the idea that the past continues to exist in the present, and that we are therefore always in the past as well as the present. Risley holds that you do not look *back* at the past as something you have left behind; instead *you look down through* different moments of a life like a series of transparencies laid one upon the other.

Chapter 2
Risley walks downtown to the gallery where her retrospective exhibition is to be held, passing modern buildings and smart shops that have appeared since she left Toronto. The sight of older ladies on the streetcars reminds her of how she and Cordelia used to criticise such people when they were high-spirited thirteen-year-olds together. They thought they were friends then. Risley is now more like the old women than the teenagers. She asks herself what she will say to Cordelia if they meet again: she wonders what Cordelia will look like. This leads to a sadistic vision of an old derelict assaulted in the street and put in an oxygen tent, and this in turn becomes a fantasy of Cordelia in an iron lung. Risley obviously feels great animosity towards Cordelia.

NOTES AND GLOSSARY:

Gabardine:	rainproof material and coat made of it
iguana:	a large lizard from South America
cerise:	cherry colour (from French), Elaine has learned the word from Mrs Finestein (p. 218)
dewlaps:	loose skin on the necks of cattle
wattles:	flesh (or lobes) hanging from the heads of fowl or fleshy animals such as pigs
iron lung:	metal casing used to maintain breathing in cases of paralysis by pumping air in and out of the cavity round the patient's body. It was invented at Harvard by Philip Drinker in 1929
polio:	poliomyelitis, a viral inflammation of the spinal cord which caused an epidemic among children in the

1950s; the iron lung was part of the treatment in extreme cases

II: Silver Paper

The painting of this name is a 'construction' (p. 348), not a proper painting, presumably made from silver paper. As a girl Elaine collects silver paper from cigarette packets to make toys (p. 27). Even as an adult, she is still on the look-out for silver paper when she walks through the park (p. 385).

Chapter 3
Risley is staying in the apartment of her former husband Jon in a commercial building on King Street. A painter, he lives by creating special effects for movies ('hacked-up body-part stuff' (p. 18)). Risley likes the apartment better than a hotel because she understands the kind of disorder in which he lives. They are both survivors of each other, 'shark . . . but also lifeboat' (p. 17).

The modern bedding (*duvet* and *futon*) makes her think about changing times in herself and in the city she is revisiting. In spite of its superficial glamour she suspects it is still the same as ever: 'Malicious, grudging, vindictive, implacable' (p. 14).

Risley talks about her life as a painter, her husband Ben, and her children Sarah and Anne. She lives in Vancouver in British Columbia to which she fled from Toronto. Ben emerges as a nice, reliable man who runs a travel agency but does not share in her experience or perspective.

She reflects on her career and what an unlikely thing it seems that she became a painter. She feels that she has had a narrow escape in doing so, though she has deep misgivings about the forthcoming exhibition with its overtones of eminence and finality – even if it is to be held in an 'alternative' gallery called Sub-Versions, run by women.

She sleeps and wakes depressed. Walking to the gallery, she encounters a poster of herself ('RISLEY IN RETROSPECT') with a moustache drawn on it, and feels cheered by the fact that she now has a face worth defacing.

NOTES AND GLOSSARY:

Futon, duvet: (*Japanese, French*) styles of bedding fashionable in the 1980s

world-class city: an expression reflecting the pride of the city in relation to political and cultural capitals elsewhere

Sub-Versions: a pun on 'subversion', the attempt to overthrow a state or authority

an old biddy: an ill-kempt and disreputable old woman (from the Irish abbreviation of 'Brigid')

IN RETROSPECT: looking back at the past; hence an exhibition covering
                   the whole career of an artist to date (also called a
                   retrospective)
Kilroy was here: generic example of graffiti, often written or spoken
                   ironically. It dates back to the Second World War,
                   when it appeared wherever the American troops had
                   been

Chapter 4

When Elaine was very young her family travelled on the highways of
northern Canada where her father, an entomologist, was doing research on
forest insects. Her earliest memories are of her parents and her brother in
the car, their ears outlined against the windscreen; of the alochol used for
collecting specimens, of the stars that seemed remote and antiseptic (like
alcohol) and Mercurochrome sunsets. Her father insists that every place
where they camp should be left as if they had never been there. There is a
war in the outside world, and they are nomads on the far edge of it because
their father is in a reserved occupation. Her brother involves her in his
play-fighting. War news filters over the radio; she suspects that their side is
losing but her brother does not think so. He sings *'Coming in on a wing
and a prayer . . .'*. This combines in her mind with her father's way of
saying, when other men are present, 'You can't fly on one wing' (p. 24).
The fights with Stephen are secret and she learns not to tell, 'loyal even in
outrage' (p. 25).

NOTES AND GLOSSARY:
LifeSavers: brand-name of a candy shaped like a ring (or life-
                   belt)
kapok: oily fibre covering the seeds of a silk-cotton tree, used
                   for stuffing pillows, sleeping bags, mattresses and so
                   on
the war: the Second World War (1939–45), in which Canadian
                   forces served as units of the British Army
Coming in on a wing and a prayer: a popular song about Royal Air Force
                   planes returning damaged after engagements with the
                   enemy. It is accredited in the prefatory notes to the
                   novel
bum: childish word for buttocks and anus (from 'bottom')
salamander: tailed amphibian resembling a lizard
Mercurochrome: antiseptic of a deep cherry-red colour
Milky Way: common name for the vast galaxy of visible stars that
                   forms a cloudy pathway in the sky
commandos: members of a special fighting unit that operates
                   behind enemy lines

Chapter 5
On her eighth birthday Elaine receives a camera with which a picture of herself outside a motel cabin is taken. She is beginning to make things out of pipe-cleaners. She collects any silver paper she finds. The schoolbooks her mother uses with her children contain stories of ordinary families that seem exotic to her: there are 'no tents, no highways, no peeing in the bushes' (p. 29), and there is no war in them. She has never met any other girls because she never stays anywhere long enough. She does not think about what she would say to one if she met her.

NOTES AND GLOSSARY:

Brownie:	brand-name of an easy-to-use camera by Kodak
motel:	drive-in hotel with cabin-type accommodation on highways
pipe-cleaners:	twisted wire and cotton used to clean pipe stems
Habitant:	referring to French-Canadian settlers and their way of life
peeing:	urinating (abbreviation of the slang word 'pissing')

Chapter 6
Elaine's family moves to a house of their own in Toronto where her father has become a professor at the university. The house is located in a 'lagoon of postwar mud' (p. 33) in a new suburb, and it is badly built, the contractor having abandoned it before the work was finished. She feels lonely.

NOTES AND GLOSSARY:

lagoon:	muddy water surrounding Venice; also enclosed sea formed by the broken ring of a volcanic island

Chapter 7
Elaine becomes familiar with the Zoology building where her father works, with its collection of stuffed animals and parts of animals such as ox eyes in formaldehyde. From the balcony, she watches the Christmas parade with its unreal Santa Claus, who is 'smaller than expected' (p. 37). Her parents have adapted to the requirements of urban life. Her mother is now wearing lipstick and a hat. The house is still in disorder.

NOTES AND GLOSSARY:

Witch of Endor:	a woman with a 'familiar spirit' or devil (see the Bible, 1 Samuel 28:7); here used as a joke
planaria:	flatworms
chitonous:	skirtlike (from Greek 'chiton')
Santa Claus:	(originally St Nicholas) patron saint of Christmas in

| | popular tradition, commonly represented as a jolly old man with a white beard, dressed in red |
| **formaldehyde:** | colourless fluid used widely to preserve museum specimens |

III: Empire Bloomers

Risley transferred Miss Lumley's bloomers to Mrs Smeath in the picture series of this name (p. 225) achieving a 'frightening symbiosis' (p. 404) of their authoritarian personalities. The bloomers in the resultant picture are said to 'radiate a dark and stifling light' (p. 226). *The Annunciation,* another picture in the series described in Chapter 41 (p. 225), shows the Smeaths having sex in the manner of insects.

Chapter 8
Risley wakes depressed, remembering previous depressions, and hears Cordelia's nine-year-old voice taunting her: *'What have you to say for yourself?'* She rings Ben, who is away in Mexico, and leaves a message. She feels unsure about the suitability of the black dress she has brought for the opening. After a jittery cup of coffee she goes out into the renovated city, full of 'multiculturalism on the march' (p. 43). In a clothes shop she prevents the theft of her wallet from her purse while trying on a dress by slamming her heel down on the offending hand – a schoolgirl's, judging by the squeals. At this point in the novel, the girl who tormented her as a child becomes a more insistent presence, and the attempted theft causes Risley to curse Cordelia (who, we learn later, would have been capable of such a prank).

NOTES AND GLOSSARY:
multiculturalism:	the conscious mixing of ethnic cultures and their traditions (cuisine and so on) in a modern city
Keep happy . . . :	see Happy Gang in Chapter 26 (p. 138)
Day-Glo:	brand-name for semi-fluorescent paint

Chapter 9
Elaine, sent to the Queen Mary Public School, is soon befriended by Carol Campbell, who shares the same bus route. The route that they take home together crosses a wooden footbridge over a ravine where dangerous men are said to lurk. For the first time Elaine is with real girls 'in the flesh' (p. 47). Carol is disdainful of primitive conditions in the Risley home, but regards her new friend as exotic. There are separate doors for BOYS and GIRLS at school, where a culture of segregation exists, although the class-rooms are in fact not divided. Carol claims that many of the boys are in love with her. Elaine sees less of her brother Stephen during school-

hours but remains friendly with him at home. She is becoming aware that 'more may be required' (p. 49) of her by her new girl-friends than she is currently able to supply.

NOTES AND GLOSSARY:

get the strap: be beaten on the hand with a leather strap

Our Lady of Perpetual Help: pietistic name for the mother of Jesus, reflecting her supposed powers of intercession

pageboy: boy servant in a royal court, hence the name for hair worn with a fringe and cut straight at the bottom

aliens: creatures from 'outer space'

Anglicans: members of the Communion of the Church of England (that is, Episcopalian Protestants)

Chapter 10

Carol is equally disgusted with the Zoology Building and its contents. Her mother wears 'twin sets' and uses a 'cold wave'. Carol introduces Elaine to her best friend, Grace Smeath, who is somewhat older. Grace's colouring books and cut-out 'ladies' from the Eaton's Catalogue become the mainstays of the girls' games. Elaine finds it easy to meet the group's requirements, such as the convention that one disparages one's own cut-out 'lady' ('My lady' (p. 53)) while actually considering it the best dressed of all.

NOTES AND GLOSSARY:

toadburgers: imaginary food based on hamburgers

cold wave: hair wave produced by the application of chemicals

Chapter 11

Elaine puts her pictures of Carol and Grace in an album that she gets for Christmas. She also gets a red plastic purse with a gold-coloured clasp. The Risleys now have a radio with a green eye on the tuning dial; it makes eerie noises between stations. There are also curtains (called 'drapes' in the American fashion) on the downstairs windows. Elaine meets Grace's mother, Mrs Smeath, who gives the impression of having a single breast descending to her waist. Mrs Smeath is said to have a bad heart, spending much time lying on a sofa. Elaine finds herself morbidly fascinated by Mrs Smeath's bad heart as she cuts out red paper hearts in class for Valentine's Day.

NOTES AND GLOSSARY:

Oxfords: sturdy big-toed shoes

Valentine's Day: lovers' feast-day when cards are exchanged (14 February)

antimacassar:	mat used to protect the back of a chair from men's hair-oil (already out-dated in the period of the chapter)
rubber plant:	tropical plant with shiny leaves that produce latex
phosphorescent:	glowing in the dark

Chapter 12

Stephen tries to build a dug-out house in the mound of earth beside their home. The girls sing skipping songs together ('*Salome was a dancer ...*' (p. 60)), Elaine climbs the ladders fearlessly on the sites of new houses now springing up around their own, and sits on the upper storeys with no floors. She is not afraid of heights, nor indeed afraid of anything. The craze for marbles reaches their school: 'cat's eyes', 'puries', 'waterbabies', 'metal bowlies', and 'aggies' are passed from winner to winner. Elaine's favourites are cat's eyes: she keeps a blue one in her red purse and does not risk it in competition. Stephen is a deadly shot and comes home with pockets bulging. He takes his winnings down into the ravine and makes a treasure map of their location.

NOTES AND GLOSSARY:

Salome:	daughter of Herodias who demanded the head of John the Baptist. The narrative is told in the Bible (see Matthew 14) although her name is given only in tradition

Chapter 13

The Risleys go north again in summer; Elaine's father is observing an infestation of caterpillars. Elaine's mother makes blueberry jelly. Elaine and Stephen explore the loggers' camp where they are staying and its surroundings, where bears roam. Stephen writes the names of stars in urine. Elaine feels disquiet when she sees her parents inside the cabin through a window: they do not know that she can see them. In September the family returns to Toronto where Elaine is confronted with a new member of the girls' circle, Cordelia. She has no premonition as she greets the new girl.

NOTES AND GLOSSARY:

turd:	faeces
premonition:	sense of things to come

Chapter 14

Elaine's name is mentioned for the first time when the other girls introduced her to Cordelia (whose second name is never given in the novel). Cordelia's family live in a new house with pastel colours, and her mother arranges flowers; the household has egg-cups, new to Elaine. Cordelia's older sisters Perdita and Miranda are said to be gifted (p. 72). They use funny, exaggerated phrases such as, 'I look like Haggis McBaggis' (p. 72).

Cordelia assumes control and the girls put on plays with the clothes her sisters have outgrown. Walking by the ravine they find deadly nightshade; Cordelia says it is a good way to poison someone. Cordelia frightens the others by talking about dead people who, she says, are dissolved in the stream that flows from the graveyard. She dares Elaine to go down beneath the bridge. Cordelia says the meals made of flowers that they lay out have been taken by the dead people.

NOTES AND GLOSSARY:
Giselle: a ballet by Adolphe Adam (1803–56). It is about the spirits of girls who die before marriage
deadly nightshade: poisonous plant from which the drug belladonna is taken
safe: rubber condom

Chapter 15
Elaine's class teacher Miss Lumley is said to wear navy-blue woollen bloomers. She beats the boys with a leather strap and expresses jingoistic views about the British Empire which, she says, brought electric lights to the dark continents (p. 79). She lauds the sterling qualities of the Royal Family during the Blitz: they are 'steadfast, loyal, courageous, heroic' (p. 80). Elaine is disturbed to think that she has to share the connotations of bloomers, at once sacrosanct and shameful, because she and Miss Lumley are both female.

NOTES AND GLOSSARY:
God Save the King: the British national anthem
Rule Britannia: patriotic song originally from the musical drama *Alfred* (1940) by Thomas Arne
Wolfe: General James Wolfe (*d.* 1759), who died taking Quebec from the French
Union Jack: British national flag formed of superimposed crosses. It appeared in the corner of flags of Commonwealth countries
sacrosanct: pertaining to the sacred and therefore the opposite of 'shameful'

IV: Deadly Nightshade

The painting of this name shows a deadly nightshade in a glass jar, with the eyes of cats barely visible in the background (p. 337). When the girls come across deadly nightshade in the ravine Cordelia identifies it as a good way to poison someone (p. 74) and later Elaine considers it as a means to commit suicide (p. 155). Throughout the novel the nightshade functions as a symbol for the poisoning of Elaine's childhood by Cordelia. Later in life, the narrator cannot remember what it was like in the grave, but when she closes her eyes she sees the tangled leaves of deadly nightshade which seem to ripple as if unseen cats were moving in them, although she knows that this memory is wrong (p. 108). At the end the nightshade has been cleared from the ravine (p. 417).

Chapter 16

Risley feels the memories of childhood closing round her and wishes she were back in Vancouver, complete with its preposterous giant slugs. She reaches the Sub-Versions gallery and views her own paintings, freshly uncrated. Among them are *Rubber Plant: The Ascension*, a study of Mrs Smeath in the *Empire Bloomers* series, painted in egg tempera (p. 86). The women running the gallery are all several times more artistic-looking than herself, with names like Charna that 'Toronto didn't used to have' (p. 87) when she lived there. Risley regards her forthcoming luncheon with Jon as merely a civilised thing to do.

Andrea, a journalist, arrives for an interview. Risley reacts acerbically to her assumptions about her reasons for painting and dissociates herself from the 'feminist' interpretation of her pictures. Nor will she give the journalist the satisfaction of telling her why she paints.

NOTES AND GLOSSARY:

cut off my ear:	as did Vincent Van Gogh (1853–90), a Dutch genius whose painting made no money while he lived but are now priceless
egg tempera:	paint made of egg yolk and pigment (see Chapter 58)
The Ascension:	Jesus 'ascended' and Mary was 'assumed' into heaven after death
doily:	lace table mat (an overly-genteel term for an overly-genteel artefact)
nifty:	British slang for clever (American 'neat')
iconoclasm:	the destruction of images for religious (or, here, ideological) reasons
knuckle-dusters:	crude weapon for punching, worn on knuckles
coda:	additional piece attached at the end of a musical composition
Viet Nam War:	(usually Vietnam) the American anti-Communist campaign in South-East Asia (1965–73)
feminism:	cultural and political movement concerned with women's rights (see below under 'Themes')

succubus: the devil assuming a female body to sleep with men (Latin approximation, 'lying underneath')

Rubens, Renoir, Picasso: respectively painters from seventeenth-century Holland, nineteenth-century France and twentieth-century Spain.

Chapter 17

Cordelia 'makes short work' (p. 92) of the cut-out ladies game and ridicules the Eaton's Catalogue from which the Smeath household is furnished. Her sisters have reached puberty: something is causing them to bulge and soften, walk rather than run. The younger girls begin to examine themselves for tell-tale signs and look at older women with morbid curiosity. There is now a wordless gulf between them and their mothers. A rumour about sex is going round, gathering horror as it goes. Cordelia supplies her friends with information about men's sexual parts (p. 94) and misinformation about human reproduction. Elaine, the daughter of a biologist, privately knows that Cordelia's terminology is erroneous. Grace declares with theological finality that God makes babies (p. 94).

NOTES AND GLOSSARY:

the curse: (*slang*) women's menstrual period

breast pumps: rubber and glass instruments used to extract milk from the human breast

ovipositors: insects' egg-laying organs

Chapter 18

The Smeaths take Elaine to church and Sunday School, neither of which she has previously attended. With them is Aunt Mildred, Mrs Smeath's sister, a former Protestant missionary in China. Elaine meets stained glass windows and their scriptural legends: 'THE KINGDOM OF GOD IS WITHIN YOU'; 'SUFFER THE LITTLE CHILDREN'; 'THE GREATEST OF THESE IS CHARITY' (p. 98). She begins to feel that her parents have been keeping things from her (like the custom of wearing hats in church), and she becomes 'suffused, with goodness' (p. 99). She memorises the scriptural text, '*The heavens declare the glory of God; and the firmament sheweth his handywork . . .*' (p. 101). The notion of the stars she derives from this is very different from the one she has learned from her scientific family: now they look watchful rather than remote. Elaine has been transported from the indifferent but kindly universe of her father to the vindictive universe of the evangelists.

NOTES AND GLOSSARY:

white bird: the Holy Spirit or Paraclete in Christian symbolism

The kingdom of God . . . : a saying of Jesus (see the Bible, Luke 17:21)

Suffer the little children: another saying of Jesus. It continues 'to come unto me and forbid them not' (see the Bible, Mark 10:14), meaning '*allow* children to approach me'

The greatest of these ...: St Paul speaking of the three theological virtues, Faith, Hope, and Charity (or Love), (see the Bible, I Corinthians 13:13)

The heavens declare ...: see the Bible, Psalms 19:1

Chapter 19

At school the girls have abandoned marbles for spoolwork (p. 102). At home Elaine reads comics in her brother's room where she is still tolerated. Stephen has fallen in love with a girl called B.W. ('Bertha Watson'), but he keeps this a secret from everyone except Elaine. He sends Elaine idiotic notes about it, making her wonder what power this girl possesses to turn her brother into a 'more nervous identical twin of himself' (p. 103). His infatuation does not last long, however, and soon he is experimenting with a chemistry set and 'collecting stars' (p. 105). He tells Elaine that the visible stars are merely echoes of the light they sent out thousands of light years ago (p. 104). His stars are evidently different from the ones in the Bible: 'they're wordless, they flame in an obliterating silence' (p. 105).

NOTES AND GLOSSARY:

spoolwork: a simple form of weaving (as described in the novel)

khaki: the yellowy-brown (or olive green) colour of field-uniforms in the British Army

bangs: American term for a hair cut straight across the forehead (English 'fringe')

Orion, the Bear ...: prominent constellations of stars which retain their fixed positions in relation to each other

Arcturus: one of the brightest stars in the Northern Hemisphere

light year: approximately 9.46×10^{12} (see also speed of light, Chapter 68)

Chapter 20

The children walk round the neighbourhood wearing fancy dress on Hallowe'en; at School they celebrate Remembrance Day with a poem ('*We are the Dead*' (p. 107)). At home, Cordelia starts digging a deep hole in her back garden; it becomes hard to get her to play at anything else. Cordelia, Grace and Carol take Elaine to the hole and lower her into it, placing wooden boards over it and shovelling earth on top of them. As soon as she realises that this is not a game she feels a sense of sadness and betrayal, then pure terror. Risley cannot exactly remember what it felt like being in the hole, only that it was full of nothing (p. 107). It was the moment when she lost her power to Cordelia (p. 107). Instead of feeling

delighted on her ninth birthday soon afterwards, she experiences a vague
sense of horror (p. 108).

NOTES AND GLOSSARY:

Hallowe'en: All Hallows' Eve (or All Souls' Night), when the
souls of the dead are supposed to revisit the world,
and a night when children collect sweets and gifts in
their neighbourhoods

Remembrance Day: commemorating the dead in the First World War

V: Wringer

The painting of this name shows a 'wringer washing machine' (p. 337) in
a disturbing shade of 'fleshtone pink' (p. 337). Elaine first imagines her
arm in the wringer (p. 123), and later imagines Mrs Smeath going through
it (p. 180). As an obvious instrument of torture, the wringer attracts
neurotic fears of torment and guilty ideas of retribution.

Chapter 21
Risley goes into Simpsons department store to stock up on food for the
apartment. Her critical eye takes in the 'disgruntled mannequins' (p. 112)
and she reflects acerbically on the religion of cosmetics with its 'Voodoo
and spells' (p. 112). In the clothes department she sees plaid dresses and
thinks about the travesty of Scottish history involved in this fashion
(p. 113). The plaid reminds her – via *Macbeth*, called 'The Tartans' by the
actors (p. 245) – of the 'endless time' (p. 113) when she was in Cordelia's
power. She remembers that she used to peel the skin off her own feet as a
symptom of the psychological distress that Cordelia caused her.

She also remembers the fears she later had for her own daughters and
the amazing faith which enables them to take security for granted. Maybe,
she thinks, girls are not so vulnerable as they used to be: nowadays it is
'more likely to be boys now with that baffled look' (p. 114). A dejected
shop attendant of her own age and Cordelia's directs her to the Food
Hall.

NOTES AND GLOSSARY:

complex ... disease: pun on 'complex', meaning both a group of buildings and a psychological condition

metastasizes: moves from one organ to another (from 'metastasis',
a term used in medicine)

plaid: American for 'tartan', associated with the Scottish
clans, who received harsh treatment from the English
government and their own aristocracy in the seventeenth and eighteenth centuries

My way of life...: from Macbeth's speech (*Macbeth*, Act V, Scene 3). *Macbeth* alternated with *Hamlet* on the Grade Thirteen syllabus in Canadian schools up to the 1960s

Chapter 22

Through the 'black door' (p. 116) of memory, Risley can see herself and the other girls watching the Christmas parade from the window-ledge of the Zoology Building. Cordelia accuses Elaine of rudeness towards her own father who has invited them and pronounces that she will have to be punished for it (p. 117). Elaine is made to stand outside Cordelia's bedroom door and when she is allowed in it seems to her that her own hand on the door-knob is strangely distant from her.

Risley narrates how she used to scan visiting friends of her daughters for signs of hypocrisy. Little girls only seem cute and small to adults; to one another they are 'life-sized' (p. 118). She recalls the sense of not being like other girls, a conviction that Cordelia would help her. Cordelia has cultivated the fiction that she does these things to her because she is her friend. Elaine fears going out to play and lingers in the kitchen at home, but she cannot call upon her mother for help: to violate the secret of her suffering at Cordelia's hands would be a terrible sin and she would be 'cast out forever' (p. 120). Risley realises that it would have been easier to have hated Cordelia (p. 120).

NOTES AND GLOSSARY:
nubbled: with lumps or balls of wool on the surface
halibut liver oil: unpleasant-tasting oil, given to children as a source of Vitamin A

Chapter 23

Cordelia sometimes turns her sadism on Carol, but she is not a suitable victim because she cries. Elaine pleads that she cannot come out to play because she has to help her mother with the washing. Her job is to run the clothes through the wringer, a piece of machinery that resembles an instrument of torture. If you ran your hand through it the blood and flesh would move up the arm in a bulge, the hand coming out the other side flattened like a glove (p. 123).

She still goes to church with the Smeaths and eats their Sunday dinners in the 'stronghold of righteousness' (p. 126). In spite of getting ten out of ten in Bible quizzes, Elaine still incurs Mrs Smeath's disapproval. Mr Smeath recites a rude ditty about beans ('the musical fruit') at the dinner table, and tries to enlist Elaine's support. Cordelia torments her later for her ignorance about the word 'toot' (p. 125). Elaine is mortified because Mr Smeath has implicated her in his vulgarity. She also feels that he is being outrageous and subversive, and therefore on the same side as Stephen when he resorts to rude words and phrases. She wonders if Cordelia should not be on that side also.

NOTES AND GLOSSARY:

dangle:	dawdle, spend time to no apparent purpose (non-standard usage)
wringer:	a domestic appliance for drying clothes by squeezing them between rolling cylinders
toot:	euphemism for 'break wind'
righteousness:	feeling of assurance that goes with conduct believed to be approved by God
subversive:	opposed to authority (see also Chapter 3)

Chapter 24
School life becomes increasingly difficult for Elaine. Cordelia plays a weasel in a production of *The Wind in the Willows*, but is indistinguishable from the other actors in her costume. Encouraged by Miss Lumley and her wooden ruler, the children learn the popular songs 'I'm Dreaming of a White Christmas', and 'Rudolph the Red-Nosed Reindeer'. Elaine knows that she will be tormented for the eccentricity of the Risley family's Christmas decorations compared with those of other families.

Mr Banerji, an Indian, one of her father's students, comes to Christmas dinner. A timid man, he is a victim of racial prejudice in Canada. Elaine finds that she can detect his misery, something she is becoming good at (p. 129). Her father and Banerji talk about the stupidity of domesticated turkeys and their flightlessness. Wild turkeys can elude practised hunters. Elaine divides her world into tame people and wild people; Carol is tame; Cordelia, however, is completely wild (p. 130).

NOTES AND GLOSSARY:

The Wind in the Willows: a classic children's novel of 1908 by Kenneth Grahame (1859–1922), it deals with the riverside adventures of Rat, Mole, Badger, and others. Stage adaptations are common

Meleagris gallopavo: Latin name for the common turkey (formerly 'guinea fowl'), a bird native to North America and domesticated in the seventeenth century

sternum: anatomical term for the breast bone
drumsticks: the thighs of an edible bird

Chapter 25
Elaine starts baby-sitting for the Finesteins, a neighbouring Jewish family. Cordelia looks upon it as demeaning work and Carol shows racial prejudice ('The Jews killed Christ' (p. 134)). Cordelia tricks Elaine into

describing her father as a 'bugger' (p. 135), instead of 'entomologist' (p. 135). Like 'kike' (p. 134), 'bugger' is a powerful word, full of ill will (p.135). She feels that she has betrayed him. She buys sweets with the money she gets from Mrs Finestein on quitting her job and shares them with the girls.

NOTES AND GLOSSARY:
ammonia-soaked: that is, soaked with urine
kikes: racist name for Jews
bugger: vulgar term for a sodomite. Cordelia is punning on 'bug', an insect (hence 'bugger', one who collects insects)

Chapter 26
Elaine is eating alphabet soup. After the girls call her out to play she vomits and is put to bed with gastro-enteritis. Wrapped in illness 'as if in cotton wool' (p. 137), she feels safe for once. After this she becomes sick quite regularly. On these occasions she stays in bed listening to the Happy Gang on the radio, a programme that fills her with anxiety. She is sceptical about the real happiness of the characters and thinks that they must be lying some of the time (p. 139). She cuts out pictures of women from *Good Housekeeping* and other magazines, gluing on different heads if she does not like the women's faces. One magazine contains a comic strip showing women doing things they should not (gossiping, being bossy, knitting excessively and so on). There is a caption saying 'This is a Watchbird watching YOU' (p. 138). She hears the Dominion Observatory Official Time signal on the radio and feels the future taking shape in the silence before the long dash. She does not want to hear it.

NOTES AND GLOSSARY:
alphabet soup: a soup for children with pasta 'letters'

Chapter 27
Elaine is ten. This spring the girls skip to a menacing song hinting at bawdiness (p. 140). It is about a lady whose house is invaded by robbers: *'Lady touch the ground . . . Lady show your shoe'* (p. 140). Marbles are back in fashion in the playground and Elaine retrieves her favourite cat's eye from a drawer. Cordelia asks what she is holding in her pocket and Elaine gets away with saying that it is just a marble. She feels that the marble has the power to protect her, and that she too can see without any emotions. It is as if she is alive in her eyes only (p. 141).

When the family's summer trip to the north is delayed Elaine feels that she will 'implode' (p. 142). On the way northwards she sees three Indians standing on the side of the road and senses her isolation (p. 142). While her parents are shopping for groceries, Elaine squashes blackflies filled with her own blood. She is recovering from Cordelia with a sense of relief but not gladness; her torn skin is growing back. At this time she enters a period of 'wordlessness' (p. 143).

The family rent a cabin on the north shore of Lake Superior. Elaine takes photographs of boulders and gives the name of cows to them (*Daisy, Elsie* (p. 203)). She comes across a decomposing raven whose shrivelled-up eye seems to be looking at her. She could torment it with a stick and it would not feel a thing because it is dead, a condition that begins to attract her. Like the marble, 'No one can get at it' (p. 144). Meanwhile Stephen is 'collecting' boat funnels on the lake. She does not join him in this since she is no longer interested in games she cannot win.

Elaine begins to have the series of dreams that will continue and modify throughout the novel: she feels as if she has 'been given permission to dream' (p. 145). She dreams that the cat's eye marble falls from the heavens and passes through her body. She dreams that the ravine bridge has become detached with her on it while her mother stands talking to other women. She dreams that the raven is hopping around with its decaying wings. She does not dream directly of Cordelia. Her mother, who is making chokeberry jelly, seems happy in their nomadic existence.

NOTES AND GLOSSARY:

National Geographic: magazine of the National Geographic Society of America containing articles and pictures that made it widely popular

marshmallow: sweet made from the root of a plant of that name

VI: Cat's Eye

The painting with this title is a self-portrait showing only the upper part of the subject's head, along with the same head, though rather younger, reflected in a mirror. In the background three small girls dressed in the 1940s winter clothes are walking in a field of snow. There are no cat's eyes – either animal or mineral – in this picture, unless the eyes of the subject resemble those of a cat (as in the cover of the Virago edition).

Chapter 28

Risley is overwhelmed by the consumerism of Simpsons department store and compares it mentally with the scuffed shoes of her childhood and the pot-roasts prepared in the pressure-cookers of her youth (p. 149). She remembers that her mother did not like housework and put the silver away in storage to avoid the labour of cleaning it. She asks herself what she would have done if she had been her mother, witnessing her scabbed lips, her bitten fingers, but realises that there were fewer choices back then. Risley goes on to speak about a painting series called *Pressure Cooker* which some critics interpreted (to her hilarity) as a feminist image of an Earth Goddess. Though the paintings do attempt to confer timelessness on her mother, like everything else in life they are 'drenched in time' (p. 151).

She finishes the cappuccino that she is drinking and makes her way homewards. She will not buy anything in the Food Hall after all; instead she will stock up at the corner store run by an Indian or a Chinese. On the way back to the apartment she is accosted by a drunken woman who mistakes her for the Blessed Virgin. She feels a fool for confusing her own softness and gullibility with goodness. She feels that she knows too much to be good: she knows herself to be 'vengeful, greedy, secretive and sly' (p. 153).

NOTES AND GLOSSARY:

pressure cooker: cooking utensil with tightly sealed lid, which shortens the cooking time
Our Lady: Catholic name for the Virgin Mary, mother of Jesus

Chapter 29

When Elaine's family returns to Toronto in September she empties of emotion, feeling as if she is being shut up in the future (p. 154). She and Carol are in Grade Five with Miss Stuart, a teacher everyone adores. Walking over the bridge she hears a voice inside her head urging her to jump. The voice is kind, not scornful; it suggests that Cordelia would be pleased if she killed herself. Elaine knows that if she told her brother he would be helpless against the indirectness of girls and would laugh at her for being a sissy. Her mother consoles her with ordinary wisdom ('Sticks and stones . . .' (p. 156)), and assures her that she does not have to play with the girls who are tormenting her. She ought to have more backbone. Elaine imagines that her spine is soft like a sardine's, which crumbles easily when you eat it. Her mother confesses that she does not know what to do about the situation, and Elaine suspects that she feels powerless too (p. 157).

NOTES AND GLOSSARY:

enthralled: brought into slavery or bondage; fascinated
Javex: brand of bleach
sissy: (*slang*) a soft and vulnerable person, especially insulting if applied to a boy
Sticks and stones . . . : proverb counselling indifference to verbal insults

Chapter 30

At school Cordelia brings in a mirror to persecute Elaine about her appearance, which is deteriorating (p. 158). The Risley parents hold bridge parties which Banerji attends, looking still more anxious. A Royal Visit by Princess Elizabeth is announced, and Elaine grasps at it in the hope it will bring about some change for her (p. 160). She places herself where the cavalcade will pass with the vaguely formulated notion of throwing herself at the Princess's mercy. The cars drive by, however, and nothing happens.

NOTES AND GLOSSARY:
flanelette: fleecy cotton cloth

Chapter 31
Miss Stuart displays murals full of people living in different parts of the world who look sunny and gay and Elaine realises that she does not have to stay where she lives for ever. When the class is asked in the art lesson to draw what they do when they go home, she draws a bed and then obliterates it with black. Miss Stuart touches her with a gesture of comprehension. On Valentine's Day Elaine gets more cards from the boys than the other girls in her class do but keeps quiet about it, hugging a secret knowledge that she can regard boys as allies (p. 163).

Carol begins to develop breasts but Cordelia is contemptuous of her 'tits'. Mr Campbell beats Carol with a belt for wearing lipstick, providing the girls with an unnerving example of the power exercised by fathers (p. 164). Carol shows her friends her mother's diaphragm, which she has found, and then the wet spot she has found on her parents' bed-linen. The girls play doctors, and Elaine is embarrassed and humiliated in a fumbling attempt to feel Carol's heart under her new breasts.

Elaine's mother is suddenly removed to hospital, leaving a blood stain on the mattress of her bed (p. 166). Her father is obviously worried. Back home and convalescent, her mother knits a single small sock before abandoning knitting. Elaine dreams that Mr Banerji and Mrs Finestein are her real parents; that her mother has twins, one a grey baby, the other lost; that the house is burnt down, and her parents have died, sinking through the hard, transparent earth, but looking up sorrowfully at her as they recede from her.

NOTES AND GLOSSARY:
smarrut, darruk:	Miss Stuart's pronunciation of 'smart' and 'dark'
crêpe paper:	kind of tissue paper that is crinkled and dyed bright colours
Woolworth's:	a department store specialising in cheap products
shortbread:	biscuit made with lots of butter
a rubber thing:	a diaphragm, a rubber cone inserted by women in the vagina to prevent pregnancy
Kleenex:	brand of tissue used for wiping (noses, etc.)

Chapter 32
The family goes to a Conversat in the Zoology Building on Saturday. On view are a human brain in formaldehyde and a turtle whose still-beating heart is visible through a hole cut in his shell; it is hooked up to a loudspeaker so the heart-beat is heard throughout the building. Elaine faints and comes to feel that she has learned something worthwhile at last: that there is a way out of places you want to leave, by 'stepping sideways, out of your own body, out of time or into another time' (p. 171).

Cordelia introduces a new torment: every time Elaine is judged or considered to have done something wrong, one of ten imaginary stacks of plates crashes; these are the equivalent of ten chances. Having been made to stand immobile by the Girls' door in the playground as a punishment, she faints and cuts her forehead. This attracts a brief show of solicitude from Cordelia. Elaine refines her fainting technique, learning to spend time outside her body without falling over (p. 173).

NOTES AND GLOSSARY:

Conversat:	an open day at a university or college (from the German)
pig Latin:	the bad Latin of schoolboys, here a secret language formed by reversing the syllables of a word and adding '-ay'

VII: Our Lady of Perpetual Help

The picture of this title ultimately owes its name to the Catholic boys' school near Queen Mary's. Elaine's brother and his friends fight against the pupils there. Later Elaine develops a devotion to the Virgin, who 'rescues' her from Cordelia (p. 189), and later still she paints the picture of her with this name, representing her as fierce and alert with yellow lion's eyes (p. 345). She does not yet know what part the Virgin played in her life when she paints it.

Chapter 33
Risley devours a slice of pizza on the way back to Jon's apartment (p. 177). She rings home and when she hears her own telephone message she leaves a 'Love you' message for Ben, who is in Mexico. The Toronto telephone book contains many Campbells, but no Risleys. There is no Hrbik either (a character shortly to appear), and no Cordelia.

Risley remembers an occasion when she was lying in bed with Jon and one of his girlfriends burst in and threw still hot spaghetti at them. She reflects that she was a long way from being able to do anything so reckless as that herself at the time but recalls admiring the girl's unabashed bad manners (p. 178).

NOTES AND GLOSSARY:
junk food: cheap food of limited nutritional value

Chapter 34

Elaine accidentally overhears Mrs Smeath and Aunt Mildred discussing her in the kitchen: they think her like a heathen, something to be expected from the daughter of her parents. Elaine feels hatred growing like a stalk in her chest (p. 180). She has found out that what she thought was a secret among the girls, their treatment of her, is actually condoned by the mother, who regards it as a punishment from God (p. 180). When Mrs Smeath notices that she has been overheard she offers no apology, only a further reproof: 'Little pitchers have big ears' (p. 180). Mrs Smeath's 'bad heart' now seems to float before Elaine like 'an evil eye' (p. 180).

Elaine considers seeking help from Jesus at Sunday School but feels that Mrs Smeath has got God completely on her side (p. 181). Grace and Cordelia accuse her of not saying the Lord's Prayer. She is loosing her religion. When she finds a garish Catholic picture of the Virgin Mary in the street she starts to pray to her privately. According to Mrs Smeath this is blasphemy: only Catholics worship the Virgin Mary and the Pope. Elaine kneels down to pray (p. 183) and her prayers are rewarded by a vision of her Virgin's heart, shown in the picture outside her chest with seven swords stuck through it. It is red, with a dark light around it, very much like Elaine's plastic purse (p. 184).

NOTES AND GLOSSARY:
ammunition: another joke about beans (see Chapter 23)
burdock: a coarse weed that grows in the ravine
pitchers: jugs (which have ears, or handles), here children. The saying means that children hear what they are not supposed to hear
God sees the little sparrow fall ...: verses based on the scriptural text, 'one of them shall not fall on the ground without your Father' (see the Bible, Matthew 10:29–31; also Luke 12:7)
Lord's Prayer: prayer taught by Jesus to his disciples (see the Bible, Matthew 6:9)
The Seven Sorrows: sorrows that 'transfixed' the heart of Mary in Catholic tradition

Chapter 35

The girls are walking home from school in Mid-March, feeling euphoric. Cordelia makes a 'snow-angel' by throwing herself on a lawn, then runs up the hill and falls when she tries to slide down. She accuses Elaine of laughing at her and, by way of punishment, throws her hat over the bridge. She tells Cordelia to go down into the ravine and collect it ('Then you'll be forgiven' (p. 187)). Elaine falls through the ice waist-deep in the freezing creek. She manages to climb out and lies on her back on the bank with specks of darkness floating before her eyes (p. 188). She senses the dead people coming up out of the water for her. On the bridge she can discern the outline of a lady. There is a glimpse of red inside her half-open cloak. It is the sacred heart of Mary. The lady says, 'You can go home now. It will be all right' (p. 189).

NOTES AND GLOSSARY:

thunk:	made-up word for the noise of contact (onomatopoeic)
creek:	(*American usage*) stream
lethargy:	sleepiness experienced by those affected by extreme cold

Chapter 36

Elaine picks herself up and reaches the path where she is met by her mother. She still finds it unthinkable to tell on Cordelia. She believes that she has seen the Virgin Mary who has listened to her prayers (p. 190). At home, she is checked by her mother for frostbite and put to bed with a fever. She dreams that she is being raised upwards by an invisible hand. Phone-calls are made, and Cordelia rings to apologise for not having waited at the bridge. Back at school, Elaine is blamed for her own parents' calls to the others' parents.

Elaine now manages to break Cordelia's spell over her. Without knowing where she finds the courage, she answers her interrogator with a denial of concern: she does not know and she does not care, she tells her (p. 193). Then she turns and walks away, resisting Cordelia's command to return: even 'Ten stacks of plates' from Carol does not frighten her into submission. It is like stepping off a cliff, believing the air would hold her up. Elaine realises that she does not have to obey Cordelia, and that she never needed to (p. 193).

In the ensuing weeks she stops going to Sunday School and refuses to play with Grace, Cordelia or Carol. Something hardens in her (p. 193). She no longer walks home by the bridge. Instead she reads her brother's comics, and makes friends with a girl called Jill who likes to play Old Maid, Snap, and other card games. Her former girl-friends recede into the background (p. 194).

NOTES AND GLOSSARY:

kernel: inside part of a nut (which is usually soft)
Kapow. Krac. Kaboom: onomatopoeic words used in comics
Old Maid, Snap, Pick Up Sticks: children's card games

VIII: Half a Face

The Risley painting of this title is the only one of Cordelia that she paints. It combines the horror story of the twins (p. 211), one of whom has only half a face, with another head in a white cloth that appears to be Cordelia's, as in Elaine's dream (p. 360). The idea that the 'twins' (Elaine and Cordelia) change places and remain tied to one another is developed in this painting and elsewhere in the text (pp. 227; 441).

Chapter 37
Elaine forms the habit of going into Catholic churches and seeking out the Virgin, but though she feels in sympathy with the 'shameless extravaganza' (p. 197) of the holy effigies, none of the statues resembles her experience.

Risley recalls a very different statue of the Virgin which she encountered in Vera Cruz, Mexico: the statue was dressed in black. On her dress were pinned little brass ornaments representing the lost things that the Virgin had 'found' for people. Risley strongly empathises with it: she herself was lost when the Virgin found her. Ben enters the church to find her on her knees, chilled through from the stone.

She now reflects on the habit her daughters had, at one time, of saying '*So?*' in answer to everything she told them – a habit that Cordelia had also. Now, when she says to Cordelia inwardly, 'You made me believe I was nothing', Cordelia seems to reply, '*So?*' (p. 199).

NOTES AND GLOSSARY:

Vera Cruz: port in eastern Mexico. The Virgin of Guadalope is the more common object of veneration in North America

So?: short for 'So what?', implying that what has been said is of no interest

Chapter 38
King George VI dies; Queen Elizabeth II ascends the throne; new stamps and coinage are introduced with her head on them. Cordelia and Grace move up to Grade Eight, but Carol and Elaine, aged eleven, are only in Grade Six. All of them are in a new school with green, eye-saving blackboards that do not screech. Elaine develops amnesia about the period that her mother describes as the bad time she had (p. 201). She does not even know that she has forgotten it. The wooden bridge is being replaced by a concrete one and this gives her the uneasy feeling that there is someone still on it, left there by mistake (p. 202). She cannot say why she feels this way since she no longer remembers her bad experience there.

Cordelia is doing poorly in class and is sent to St Sebastian's, a private school, instead. Carol stays on but is not popular with other girls; she hangs around with boys during recess and runs in a 'funny wiggling way' (p. 202). Elaine has a boyfriend who is beaten at school and is generally admired for it. Elaine sees television, now becoming widespread, for the first time (p. 202).

Soon Carol too moves away, and Elaine (now twelve) goes on to Grade Eight. She cuts her hair and reorganises the cupboard in her bedroom, finding the red purse and the cat's eye marble in the process. She puts the marble in the purse and deposits it in the trunk in the cellar. She does not like thinking about things closely connected with her life as a child. She is now tired of childhood and ready for high school (p. 203).

Cordelia's mother rings to know if Elaine would like to meet her daughter, who is moving to the same high school. She has been expelled from St Sebastian's (as Cordelia later explains) for drawing a penis on a wall-chart of a bat. She has also added the name of a male teacher. Elaine does not speak to her but agrees to meet.

Cordelia is already practised in the flippancy which goes with high school. She has grown rangy and heavier; she has breasts and a pony-tail, and her hair has a peroxide streak. Elaine remembers nothing of the past and is impressed by Cordelia's sophistication, but also apprehensive. She wonders if she will end up the same way as Cordelia, failing exams and drawing penises on bats.

NOTES AND GLOSSARY:

George VI:	died on 6 February 1952. Princess Elizabeth was crowned Queen on 2 June 1953. The coronation was televised
happy as a clam:	a 'smile' is formed by the meeting 'lips' of the shell of a mollusc of this kind
pony-tail:	hair gathered together at the back
peroxide:	used to make hair blond by bleaching action
rangy:	slender and long-legged; an American usage originally meaning capable of long journeys on the range

Chapter 39
Mr MacLeod, head of Burnham High School, considers himself a kinsman of Dame Flora MacLeod of Dunvegan Castle in Scotland, and encourages the students to regard it as their ancestral home. The girls in Elaine's year are reaching puberty and acquiring breasts and faces 'slick with oily juice' (p. 207). Elaine despises them when they start 'squealing and flinging themselves around' (p. 207). Many of the boys are 'gigantic' (p. 207). Boys can be 'pills' or creeps, but others, according to Cordelia,

are 'dreamboats' – a term that Elaine has a good deal of difficulty understanding. The two girls make what they consider to be witty remarks to one another. They are embarking on the period described at the beginning of the novel (p. 4).

Their taste in clothes is partly gleaned from Cordelia's sisters, Perdie and Mirrie, though what Cordelia considers 'sharp' they are likely to consider 'cheap' (p. 109). It is clear from what they say that Cordelia still has a problem with her father. When she answers them back, they remind her what he said the last time. Cordelia, who does not have an answer, flushes at this (p. 210).

She starts 'pinching' things such as horror comics from shops. The girls examine these with morbid fascination. There is a story about two sisters, one of whom has facial burns and hangs herself, but the other is pretty and has a boyfriend. The dead girl's spirit gets into a mirror and when the other girl looks at it, it takes possession of her body. In the end the boyfriend breaks the mirror (p. 211). Elaine is unable to sleep with the comics in her room and adds them to her brother's collection.

NOTES AND GLOSSARY:

Burnham: Birnam Wood is a place-name associated with the witches' prophecy in *Macbeth* (see Chapter 44)

dreamboat: possible corruption of 'dream beau', meaning an ideal imaginary suitor

pinching: (*slang*) shop-lifting; literally, painful pressure applied between thumb and finger

puke: vomit; a term of contempt reserved for gross sentimentality or trashy sensationalism

Chapter 40
Elaine is in Ninth Grade. The Risleys listen to the comedian Jack Benny on their new radio set in its blond wooden cabinet. The furniture, all Scandinavian, has been selected by Elaine's father since her mother is uninterested in such matters. To her daughter's mortification, she has taken up ice-dancing; yet Elaine also admires her 'don't-give-a-hoot' (p. 214) attitude. Stephen has won a scholarship to a private school for 'brainy boys' (p. 215). Elaine is offered a private school if she wants one but the idea of being locked up in a boarding-school with only girls fills her with fear (p. 215).

Stephen is required to wear an English choirboy's haircut and looks like an illustration from a 1920s adventure-book. He swops clever insults with his friends across the chess board (p. 215) and discusses the future of the world with his father (p. 216). Mr Risley believes that the methane produced by cows bred in vast numbers to supply insulin for diabetics will destroy the ozone layer. Stephen takes a long-range view. He regards life on earth as insignificant in relation to the immensity of the universe (p. 217).

From their argument, Elaine gathers that 'Who ever cares the most will lose' (p. 217). Her own heart hardens towards the human race. She believes that knowing too much about others will put you in their power (p. 217). She particularly dislikes knowing about her father's life before his marriage (p. 217). She concentrates on Home Economics.

Sometimes Stephen and Elaine still double over with laughter at invented words ('Frut', 'pronk' (p. 218)). Stephen shares some of his knowledge about the universe: 'there are no such things as discrete objects which remain unchanged, set apart from the flow of time' (p. 219). It strikes Elaine that his theory makes everything seem as if it were made of solid light (p. 220). He tells her that if one of a pair of twins were rocketed into space fast enough he would return ten years younger than the other. Elaine thinks this would be sad. She sees also some menace in his notion of time-travel which she cannot pin down.

Stephen works in a boys' camp during this summer and writes her letters reporting on the fellow camp instructors' drooling, girl-inspired imbecility. Cordelia writes letters full of affected boredom. Elaine feels as if she is 'marking time' (p. 221), a phrase that echoes Stephen's assertion that space–time is 'what we live in' (p. 219). She finds her parents too cheerful.

NOTES AND GLOSSARY:

doesn't-give-a-hoot: is completely indifferent (a hoot being a derisory noise)

flannels: casual woollen trousers

claustrophobic: afraid of being closed in

diabetic: suffer from diabetes, a disease caused by the failure of the pancreas to produce insulin. Animal insulin was isolated in 1921; pigs are now the preferred source

greenhouse: glass-house for growing vegetables. The 'greenhouse effect' is said to be produced by human interference with the earth's atmosphere. Excessive methane (CH_4), destroys the ozone layer around the earth (O_2)

Möbius strip: invented by August Ferdinand Möbius (1798–1868), who pioneered the use of projective geometry in physics

Klein bottle: invented by Felix Klein (1849–1925), a pioneer of non-Euclidean physics

biceps: largest muscle-group on the upper arm (an obvious measure of virility)

crackers: water biscuits

IX: Leprosy

In the painting of this name the subject is sitting in front of a mirror with half her face peeling off; she is like the villain in a horror comic that Elaine once read (p. 352). A popular song of this name which the girls parody in high school days is given in Chapter 42. A key line, 'Night and day you torture me' (p. 229), is behind the painting though Elaine does not recognise its relevance to her relationship with Cordelia. Probably she does not understand her reason for depicting a 'leper' either when she does the painting.

Chapter 41
Charna rings enthusiastically from the gallery to report on the coverage the exhibition is getting in the newspaper's Entertainment Section, where Andrea's interview has appeared ('CROTCHETY ARTIST STILL HAS POWER TO DISTURB' (p.225)) along with a photograph of herself and two paintings from the *Empire Bloomers* series. Risley comments that the black and white photos cannot do justice to the intense indigo blue that radiates a dark and stifling light in the original painting (p. 225). To her annoyance the interviewer uses the words 'eminent' and 'post-feminist' (p. 226).

Risley feels sure that Cordelia will recognise Mrs Smeath from the newspaper pictures; then she will come to the opening and see herself in *Half a Face*. Risley wanted the eyes to be those of a thirteen-year-old girl, belligerent as Cordelia's were then, but they turned out frightened instead. She reflects that she is less afraid of seeing Cordelia than of *being* Cordelia, for she believes that in some way they have actually 'changed places' (p. 227).

NOTES AND GLOSSARY:

Leprosy:	a disfiguring disease in which the extremities of the body are progressively lost due to lack of feeling (fingers, toes, nose etc.)
rave:	(*slang*) respond enthusiastically (from the word for feverish talk)
mausoleum:	magnificent tomb (see also Chapter 42 (p. 232))
post-feminist:	an intellectual position based on a feminist outlook (see Chapter 16) modified by the recognition that it is in fact 'a position'

Chapter 42
Elaine is now in Grade Ten and has entered puberty: when menstruating, she is entitled to sit out volley-ball games and go to the nurse for aspirin and sanitary towels. Cordelia is increasingly unmanageable at school. She

is caught smoking, and Risley reflects that it must have been difficult for the teachers to understand why the pair were friends.

On the way home from school Cordelia throws herself down in the snow and this stirs up an uncomfortable feeling in Elaine. Together they start ridiculing Grace Smeath and her family as the Lump-lump Family (p. 230). Elaine recognises the treachery in all of this, since when they were girls Grace was admired by them all (p. 231). At the same time it is deeply satisfying.

The girls walk into the cemetery from where they have a view of the Smeath family home. Elaine has a quick memory of the bridge and the creek, but immediately represses it. She joins Cordelia in ridiculing the Eaton family's mausoleum (p. 232). Elaine tells Cordelia that she herself is a vampire, and when she refuses to admit it is a joke Cordelia becomes uneasy. This gives Elaine a sense of malevolent triumph and she now knows that she is the stronger of the two of them (p. 233).

NOTES AND GLOSSARY:
highball: a cocktail drink
parodies: comic versions of songs usually arrived at by altering
                     individual words

Chapter 43
Elaine is in Eleventh Grade and wears the current fashions, flared at the top and skinny at the bottom (p. 234). She has developed a 'mean mouth' (p. 234) and makes cutting remarks to other girls, though not to boys. This is dangerous but it wins her a kind of admiration. She uses Cordelia for target practice.

One day when she is doodling in History class she draws the face of the girl sitting across from her. The History teacher is talking passionately about the Second World War, which he regards as the end of an era (p. 236). Elaine finds it hard to believe she was alive at the time. Women wore padded shoulders and nipped-in waists with peplums (p. 236). She draws a woman with wide shoulders and a picture hat. She finds the hands hardest, but has begun to draw.

Elaine has boyfriends now. She seems to understand their needs; with girls she feels more awkward. She understands that boys need silences; that they are apprehensive about their own physical nature (p. 237). She conducts lingering conversations with them on the phone, mostly composed of silence.

Parents are now a liability who seem like children and blurt out humiliating things. She does not mope about love, like girls in magazines. Risley reflects that her love for boys was visual (that of a painter in the making); she wanted to possess their bodies through the eyes. This has only partly to do with sex: she sees the body as being made of energy, a form of solidified light (p. 240), another idea that echoes Stephen's theory of the universe (p. 220).

NOTES AND GLOSSARY:

Anschluss: annexation of Austria by Germany in 1938

peplums: short skirt-like section at he back of a jacket, part of the post-war New Look

broad: (*American slang*) attractive woman

necking: protracted kissing, a relatively intense form of physical courtship

corsages: arrangements of flowers to be worn on the breast

Chapter 44

A girl is murdered in a ravine. To Elaine it seems terribly unfair that the victim should go into the realm of the 'not mentionable' (p. 241) as though it were her own fault that she was murdered. The bad men said to lurk in the ravine now seem more real to Elaine.

She coaches Cordelia for an exam, but Cordelia cannot concentrate; instead she ridicules her teachers. Cordelia herself is easy to ridicule now: Stephen says that she 'has a tendency to exist' (p. 242), just as atoms have. Elaine and Cordelia go out together on double dates (p. 243) with boys, but Cordelia does not understand how to cope with male silence, and she frightens them off. Besides, she is not at all interested in what they have to say (p. 243).

When the Earle Grey players come to Toronto Cordelia appears as an extra in *Macbeth*. She substitutes a fresh cabbage for the rotten one used as Macbeth's head in the last scene and it bounces noisily off the stage. Although she seems to laugh off her mistake, she is deeply unsettled by it.

In Grade Thirteen Elaine helps Cordelia with her Zoology but Cordelia is too squeamish to do dissections (p. 247). Cordelia's father brings his 'ponderous, ironic, terrifying charm' (p. 249) to bear on Elaine when she visits. She notices that Cordelia's fumbled efforts to appease him do not work because she is too frightened. Nothing Cordelia can do or say will ever be enough: 'she is somehow the wrong person' (p. 249).

Elaine dreams about boys; she also dreams she is in an iron lung. In other dreams someone is watching her in a mirror, and a red purse full of treasure bursts and spews dead frogs. There is also a head wrapped in a tea-towel that she dares not unwrap because it will come alive.

NOTES AND GLOSSARY:

$E=mc^2$: formula created by Albert Einstein (1879–1955) in his general theory of relativity. It establishes the equivalence of mass and energy and explains movement and gravitation in relation to it

double dates: two boys and girls together, usually when the couples
                     are not 'serious' about each other
Earle Grey: a fictitious theatrical company; there is, however, an
                     English tea called Earl Grey
Julius Caesar, Macbeth: tragedies by William Shakespeare (1564–1616)
mushier: more mushy, 'soft', or sentimental; literally having
                     the quality of much-boiled food

Chapter 45
Cordelia and Elaine are in Sunnysides diner drinking vanilla milkshakes.
Cordelia mentions her own faked illness as a child (p. 251). She talks
about the holes she used to dig in the back garden and explains she did it
to have a place where no one could disturb her (p. 252). When she was
little she used to get into trouble with her father. She hated moving house,
hated Queen Mary's and had no friends there except Elaine.

For Elaine it seems as if Cordelia's face suddenly dissolves, her nine-
year-old face taking shape beneath it with a clear revelation of what
has really been there all along (pp. 252–3). Elaine feels an all-pervading
sense of shame, guilt and terror, but she does not know where these
emotions come from and she does not want to know. Inside her head there
is a 'square of darkness, and purple flowers' (p. 253). The first is the
grave in which Cordelia buried her; the second are flowers of the deadly
nightshade.

NOTES AND GLOSSARY:
Sunnysides: that is, 'sunny side up', used of eggs fried on one side
                     only
bug me: (*slang*) annoy me

Chapter 46
Elaine starts avoiding Cordelia without knowing why. She shrugs off
friendly enquiries on the phone (p. 254). Cordelia fails more tests and
changes school again, then her family moves away.

Time passes. Elaine is sitting the final Grade Thirteen exams. She does
well in the Biology exams. In the middle of the Botany paper it comes to
her that she is going to be a painter, not a biologist. Suddenly and silently,
her life has changed (p. 255).

Soon after that, she receives a call from Cordelia asking her to visit. She
finds Cordelia pasty and overweight; 'Things are bad for her' (p. 256). She
has a tutor called Miss Dingle, but it is obvious that she will not pass
the entrance exams for university. Though hopelessly uninterested in her
future she recognises a betrayal in Elaine's suggestion that she ought to
consider secretarial school.

Cordelia wants to talk about their time together as thirteen-year-olds, when they thought they were wonderful (p. 258). Elaine is afraid of where such memories will lead her and hardens against her: Cordelia is acting stupidly; all she lacks is will-power (p. 258). Elaine wants to escape before Cordelia's mother arrives to look at her reproachfully. Why should she endure that for something that is not her fault? As she leaves she sees Cordelia's face behind the front window.

NOTES AND GLOSSARY:

ritzier:	'posher', better-off (from the Ritz, a celebrated hotel in New York)
raceme, rhizome:	terms in botany respectively for stems producing flowers at the top and for stems that grow underground with roots and leaves branching off them
photosynthesis:	process by which plants convert carbon into tissue using sunlight and releasing oxygen
Scrofulariaciae:	monopetal plants of the fig-wort family (commonly -ph- for -f-)
legumes:	generic term for beans, peas and so on
jerk:	slang for a worthless person (from 'jerk off', to masturbate)

X: Life Drawing

The painting of this name, described in Chapter 64, shows Josef and Jon, both naked and viewed from behind, painting very different images of a nude woman who has a sphere of bluish glass for a head (pp. 365–6). The painting epitomises the attitude towards art and women of the two men with whom Elaine had relationships in college. The model is presumably herself, with a cat's eye marble head. Their respective canvasses show a pre-Raphaelite model and a series of 'intestinal swirls' (p. 366).

Chapter 47
Risley wonders which of the diseases of the memory she will suffer from later on (for she is sure she will suffer from one of them). She goes out to meet Jon for lunch at the Quasi restaurant; it is his choice. He is going to be late as ever, though in the event he is not so late as she expected. The restaurant is decorated in 'ultra-black' and occupied by young people.

Someone who looks like Cordelia passes, but it is not she. Risley wonders why Cordelia's parents called her after the third sister in *King Lear* (p. 263). Would things have been different if she had been called Jane? She now sees her own name 'Elaine', which she did not like at first, as tough and pliable (p. 263).

Jon arrives and they exchange some repartee about their respective marital partners and their advancing age. His work making movie props is going well; his 'art' is not. They talk about their daughter Sarah, then briefly discuss the interview with Risley in the paper (p. 265). Risley recalls the violence of their marriage but finds herself fonder of him now than of some other past lovers (p. 266). Jon is mellower than he was: he is currently living apart from his second wife and admits that he is partly to blame (p. 266). Risley wonders if men should ever have been told about their humanity since it has made them so uncomfortable, and so much more difficult to read. She feels that forgiving men is easier than forgiving women (p. 267).

Walking back to the apartment alone she thinks about *Falling Women*, her painting that shows women who have hurt themselves by falling onto men (p. 268) – not been hurt by men, because men are a natural force, not to be blamed for such accidents. This becomes the departure point for the sections of the novel that reconstruct her relationships with Hrbik and with Jon.

NOTES AND GLOSSARY:

diseases of the memory: amnesia; the diseases she refers to are concerned with disrupted speech behaviour (also called aphasia)
foreign language: Latin and Italian
The third sister: Cordelia is the youngest of King Lear's daughters in Shakespeare's play, and the only one who truly loves him
shelf-life: recommended period for storage after which a product is too old for sale
hatchet-job: a savage review or interview
technicolour: from Technicolor, brand-name for standard colour film process in the cinema since the 1950s
risqué: bordering on the indecent (from French, 'to take a risk')
fallen women: Victorian phrase for women known to have had extra-marital sex, especially prostitutes

Chapter 48
Elaine has graduated from High School and gone on to university with a scholarship earned in Biology. She is studying Art and Archeology, a combination that her parents can just about tolerate, but she is also taking night classes in life drawing at the Toronto College of Art, along with two other young women, two older women and eight young men including Jon and Colin. To qualify for the course she had to present her portfolio to the teacher, Josef Hrbik (p. 271). A Hungarian refugee in his thirties, he believes in tactile values and passion in art, and holds somewhat similar opinions about life. He tells Elaine, 'You are an unfinished *voman*, but here you will be finished' (p. 273).

NOTES AND GLOSSARY:

Moonlight Sonata: popular name for Opus 27, No. 2 by Ludwig van Beethoven (1770–1827), a perennially popular piece of piano music

Muskoka: a town north of Toronto and its chief holiday resort

Chapter 49

Art lectures at the university run through the ages starting with the classical period. Elaine finds the continually broken body parts of the statues demoralising but is surprised to learn that the originals were brightly coloured, even dressed in real clothing. None of the students on the course want to be artists. Several of the girls want to teach art, or else (in one case) to become a curator. The rest are vague about their plans, meaning that they intend to marry before it becomes necessary to find work (p. 275). Classes in life drawing would seem ridiculous to them. Elaine begins to wear the black turtlenecks and jeans of art school students and beatniks, Mrs Finestein tells her mother that she is 'letting herself go' (p. 277). Elaine agrees: she is *letting herself go* (p. 277).

NOTES AND GLOSSARY:

turtlenecks: sweaters with soft rolled collars (also 'polo necks')

beatniks: name adopted by (and for) young artists and writers in the 1950s and the early 1960s

entablatures: the flat ceiling of a porch in a Greek temple resting on columns and above which the pediment is raised. The features of classical architecture are called 'orders'

Chapter 50

Elaine goes out with the men in her Life Drawing class who need her company in order to be allowed to enter the more pleasant ladies' sections of the local beer parlours. She has suddenly acquired a new idea of male attractiveness (p. 279), but the students are too young and callow to match up to it. They treat her as an honorary member of their club, discussing their girl-friends in front of her without restraint.

As modern painters they are opposed to life drawing. They distrust words: real painters grunt like Marlon Brando (p. 279). They want to get to New York, holding that Paris and London are finished as centres of painting, and that Toronto is 'a dump' (p. 280).

They like to make fun of Mr Hrbik, whom they call 'Uncle Joe', although everyone knows he escaped from Eastern Europe during the Hungarian Revolution (p. 281). Susie, one of the other two girls, leaps to Hrbik's defence: he is not old, merely thirty-five (p. 282). But how does she know?

NOTES AND GLOSSARY:

Marlon Brando: method actor, famous for his sullen performances in *The Wild One* (1954) and other films of the period
Uncle Joe: the name familiarly given to Josef Stalin, dictator of Soviet Russia, who died in 1953
Hungarian Revolution: 1956, when Hungarian independence was crushed by Soviet tanks
D.P.: 'displaced person', a contemporary term for refugees admitted to Canada on political asylum

Chapter 51
The Art and Archaeology lecturer at the university has finished with the medieval period by February. There is an abundance of Virgin Marys during the Renaissance, though 'Jesus has trouble looking like a real baby' (p. 283).

At night classes, Elaine becomes convinced that Susie is having an affair with Hrbik. The more Susie is suspected, the less she is able to keep quiet about him. She tells the class that he had a wife who would not come with him and two daughters whom he misses (p. 285). Elaine decides that Hrbik is *'besotted'* with Susie (p. 285). Susie is the calculating one; she is too shallow to be capable of love. Elaine has a feeling that Hrbik needs rescuing. She does not yet know that a man can be admirable in some ways but not in others (p. 286).

NOTES AND GLOSSARY:

reliquaries: ornate containers for saints' relics, often in the shape of the body part within
Renaissance: the period from the mid-fifteenth century when European culture was characterised by an increasing secular humanism, stimulated by rediscovery of the classics
besotted: literally drunken; infatuated

Chapter 52
Unlike Susie, Elaine still lives at home. Her bedroom is decorated with Beckett and Sartre posters. Her mother thinks she is not getting enough sleep (which is true). Her father treats her as a biologist and feeds her information from the world of science. Stephen is now studying astrophysics at a university in California. While following exotic butterflies in a fenced off area he is arrested by the military and, on being released from custody, finds that his bicycle has been stolen. According to his letters to Elaine, he is hard at work on The Nature Of The Universe: is it an ever-enlarging blimp or a pulsating mass? This is the central question (p. 290). She feels that he no longer knows whom he is writing to, she has

changed so much. Also, she suspects that he thinks he is safe because 'he is who he says he is' (p. 291). In reality he is 'out in the open, and surrounded by strangers' (p. 291).

NOTES AND GLOSSARY:

Waiting for Godot:	play (1953) by Samuel Beckett (1906–89) which came to epitomise the futility of existence for the post-war generation
No Exit:	play by Jean-Paul Sartre (1905–80), the leading existentialist philosopher
algae:	simple forms of plant-life that live in water
blimp:	non-technical word referring to a dot on a radar screen
cod liver oil pills:	taken for vitamin A

Chapter 53
Elaine sees Susie emerge in tears from Hrbik's office during student evaluations. When she goes in after her, Hrbik draws her down between his knees and kisses her. She is about to embark on a new phase of her life: there will be no more groping in car seats, no more experimentation (p. 294). They take a taxi to his apartment on Hazelton Avenue where he lives in a near-slum: there she loses her virginity on a mattress covered with a rough Mexican blanket.

Elaine takes a job at the Swiss Chalet on Bloor Street, and shares an apartment nearby with two other students. She is seeing Josef two nights a week. On other nights he sees Susie, who cooks for him. Josef says that Susie must not know about Elaine because this would hurt her terribly (p. 296). Susie wants him to marry her, he says, implying that this is unreasonable. Elaine herself believes that marriage is a crude exchange (p. 297). Susie talks about Hrbik and herself together and Elaine continues to be friendly with her, though a little wary. On days off from work, Elaine tries to draw the furniture in her apartment though sometimes she just reads mystery murders in the bathtub.

Josef will not talk about his war experience (he later confides that he once shot a man in the head (p. 305)). He tells Elaine his dreams about women wrapped in cellophane, none of whom are her, but he also tells her that she is his 'country' now that Hungary has ceased to exist for him (p. 299).

Elaine is under stress at the Swiss Chalet where the air-conditioning has broken down. She is having dinner with Josef at the Chaumière restaurant, eating tinned snails, when it suddenly strikes her that she is miserable.

NOTES AND GLOSSARY:
smell of rubber: presumably Hrbik is using a condom

Swiss Chalet:	American restaurant chain
knocked up:	(*slang*) made pregnant
spectre:	ghost, or threat. Compare 'the spectre of Communism'
cellophane:	transparent synthetic wrapping material (originally a brand-name)

Chapter 54

Cordelia gets in touch, saying that she has run away from home (p. 300). She is thinner. For the first time in her life she is looking distinguished, if not beautiful. She is working at the Stratford Shakespearean Festival managed by Tyrone Guthrie. She talks about the problems of acting in the round. Elaine is impressed, though she is unwilling to revisit past events with Cordelia and tells her nothing about her own present way of life. She is unnerved by Cordelia's admission that what she liked best was shoplifting (p. 303), and feels diminished to see her tiny reflection in the mirror-glasses that Cordelia puts on. She accepts a free ticket to *The Tempest*, but it is impossible to distinguish Cordelia in her costume.

NOTES AND GLOSSARY:

Stratford Shakespearean Festival: founded at Stratford-on-Avon, Ontario, during the early 1950s by Sir Tyrone Guthrie (1900–71) who pioneered 'acting in the round'

The Tempest, Richard III, Measure for Measure: plays by William Shakespeare (see p. 41)

Then if you speak . . . : from an eight-line speech uttered by Francisca, a nun, in *Measure for Measure* (Act I, Scene 4, lines 12–13)

Chapter 55

Josef makes Elaine dress like a pre-Raphaelite model in a flowing purple robe with her hair loosened. He takes her to the Plaza Park Hotel Roof Garden and tells her over dinner that he hates life drawing and that he wants to direct films. Hungarians in the film industry in the United States will help him: Toronto lacks a soul (p. 305). He tells Elaine that he once shot a man in the head during the Revolution in Hungary, declaring mournfully that his country no longer exists, and that hers does not yet exist. His love-making has become ruminative as if his mind is on something else (p. 305).

Jon comes to the Swiss Chalet and asks her to go for a drink. She takes a shower before meeting in the Maple Leaf. They talk about Josef, who has not been seen. 'He's probably in Susie's knickers' (p. 307), says Jon, treating her like an honorary boy. When they leave, Elaine finds herself crying. He walks her back to his apartment. They fall onto the floor together and make love.

NOTES AND GLOSSARY:
Manhattans: cocktails made of whiskey and vermouth
knickers: contemporary (and now old-fashioned) English word
                    for women's underpants
fruit: slang for homosexual

XI: Falling Women

This painting is described and explained in Chapter 47. It shows three
women falling off a bridge onto men who are lying below like unseen
rocks (p. 268). Here 'falling' is fruitfully confused with 'fallen' in a kind
of Freudian slip. This is the painting that Risley's young admirer in the
gallery likes best because it seems to sum up an era (p. 412). For her it is a
feminist image, though for Risley the men are no more to be blamed
for hurting women than the weather: they are 'mindless as blizzards'
(p. 268).

Chapter 56
Risley walks back to the apartment past the South African War memorial
with its large female figure representing Victory or Death. She wonders
if anyone remembers that war now. The Zoology Building has been
demolished and the ledge where she sat watching the Christmas parade is
empty air: does anyone else remember it? She walks into Josef's old
neighbourhood and remembers his slow love-making on summer evenings
(p. 312). She knows more about Josef now, his desperation, his emptiness.
What was he doing with two women fifteen years younger than himself? If
one of her daughters fell in love with such a man, she would be frantic.
She thinks of the flasher her daughter once saw. Faced with modern
society, she is now capable of being shocked and fearful for her children as
she would not be for herself (p. 313).
   As she walks she is accosted by a young middle-eastern woman who
asks for money. The woman speaks of her country where there are many
people being killed (p. 314). This is the war that killed Stephen, Risley
reflects (an event still to be narrated). She gives the woman some money,
thinking it obscene to have so much power and to feel so powerless.

NOTES AND GLOSSARY:
puttees: cloth strips wound round legs from ankle to knee,
                        part of British Army uniform in the South African
                        War and the First World War (1914–18)
South African War: fought between Britain and the Boers (1899–1902)
Victorian dowager: Queen Victoria (though strictly speaking a dowager is
                        the widow who holds land or title from her husband)
just deserts: the restaurant is evidently called 'Just Desserts'

flasher:	man who exposes his sexual parts in public
wimple:	a stiff cloth enclosing the head, ears, cheeks and neck, worn by women in medieval Europe and still worn by nuns
Allah:	Arabic name for God. Elaine thinks the woman is being insincere when she uses the English word instead of one used in Islam

Chapter 57

Elaine is seeing both Josef and Jon throughout September. She has stopped working at the Chalet and is living at home again, in the basement. Josef tells her that women belong to men where he comes from and talks about violent acts of jealousy, though it is clear that he does not know about Jon. She suspects there is something silly about Josef but she cannot see him objectively.

For Elaine Jon represents things she needs at present: 'escape . . . fun, and mess' (p. 316). His love-making is 'rambunctious' (p. 318). He paints in violent, eye-burning acrylic loops and swirls. His paintings are not about anything, they are moments in a process, pure art. He would think less of her if he knew about Josef.

Susie visits the Swiss Chalet before Elaine has left to ask if she has seen Josef. She is looking poorly. Elaine lies badly (p. 319). Later Susie telephones her and asks her to come over. Elaine arrives to find her haemorrhaging heavily and gets her to the hospital. Elaine is horrified by the mismanaged abortion but also hears a meaner voice inside her head saying '*It serves her right*' (p. 321).

Josef is anguished and Elaine realises that he always sees women in relation to himself; regarding them as 'inert and innocent' (p. 321) in themselves. Without Susie his dependency on Elaine is too heavy to bear and his misery makes her feel ruthless. She stops seeing him. Josef accosts her outside the museum and tells her that she is driving him to despair. 'Good,' she answers, and finds walking away from him 'enormously pleasing' (p. 322).

NOTES AND GLOSSARY:

acrylics:	synthetic paints of great brilliance
rambunctious:	unruly
knitting needle:	sometimes used to terminate pregnancies in 'back-street' abortions. Abortion was illegal at the time
popsicle:	frozen flavoured water on a stick ('ice-pop')

Chapter 58

Susie and Josef fade from Elaine's life. She decides that she is in love with Jon. Their existence together involves turtle-necks, parties, folk-songs, marijuana ('dope' and 'pot'); they are a couple although nothing has been said explicitly. Jon believes that sexual possessiveness is bourgeois. He is now doing eye-hurting paintings with lines and circles, calling them *Enigma*, or *Variation*, or *Opus*.

In Art and Archaeology the lecturer has moved on through the Renaissance to the Baroque period. There are still Madonnas and saints, but murkier, and biblical subjects are beginning to be more violent (p. 325). Thereafter appear in order ships by themselves; animals by themselves; peasants by themselves; landscapes, flowers, lobsters and naked women. The naked women are presented in the same manner as the lobsters (p. 326).

Elaine begins to paint in egg tempera, an early Renaissance technique. She cooks up gesso in the kitchen at home; the tempera often goes bad and stinks. She concentrates on effects of glass and light-reflecting surfaces such as bottles and earrings, and studies *The Arnolfini Marriage* by Van Eyck. At the same time she starts taking night classes in commercial art, taught by an elderly Yugoslav who specialises in smiles and once had a great success with a famous illustration for canned pork. Jon calls him 'Mr Beanie-Weenie' (p. 328).

NOTES AND GLOSSARY:

egg tempera, gesso: method of painting using egg yolk, to bind the pigment, and gesso (plaster), to provide an absorbent base. Early Renaissance painters who used it included Cimabue, Giotto, and later Botticelli, and others

Johannes Van Eyck: Dutch painter (1390–1441). Earliest exponent of a style in which picturesque compositions were abandoned in favour of realistic pictures reflecting the prestige of the newly emerging merchant class. In *The Arnolfini Marriage*, the mirror at the rear is round and somewhat spherical. The wife looks heavily pregnant, though this may be due to her high-waisted dress

Norman Rockwell: an American illustrator (1894–1978) who produced magazine covers that idealised (white, middle-class) American family life. These came to be disparaged for their sentimentality and conservatism

Chapter 59
Elaine graduates from university, taking four credits in commercial art from the Toronto Art College night school as well as life drawing. She cuts her hair and carries her portfolio around potential employers, and eventually gets a job doing mock-ups. She finds a small apartment in a

crumbling house. Jon ridicules the magazine look that she manages to impose on it but he visits her there often.

Her parents sell their house and move north where her father takes a research post. Elaine does not miss them. She gets promotion at work and then moves to a publishing company designing covers. She paints at night and is often groggy in the daytime but nobody seems to notice.

Her parents send her postcards. Her brother writes from Germany and other foreign places; then from San Francisco with news of his marriage; then from New York with news of his divorce (p. 331). Elaine attends a lecture that he gives in Toronto on 'The First Picoseconds and the Quest for the Unified Field Theory'. He looks extremely clever but at the same time he has a crumpled and puzzled appearance (p. 331). Elaine's recollection of their shared childhood contains a gap of two years after which he appears again on the other side, inexplicably older by two years (p. 333).

NOTES AND GLOSSARY:

particle accelerator: large-scale scientific laboratory used in nuclear physics

Piceseconds: infinitesimally small units of time

Munchkins: elfish little people in the popular American children's story *The Wonderful Wizard of Oz* by L. Frank Baum (1856–1919)

Unified Field Theory: combining quantum theory and Einstein's general theory of relativity (see Chapter 44)

fiat lux: 'let there be light', the words with which God created the world in the Latin translation of the Bible (Genesis 1:3)

Chapter 60

Jon's paintings are now like commercial illustrations. He spends more time at her place since his apartment is full of American draft-dodgers. Elaine is slipping into a domestic role and even takes his washing to the laundromat. She discovers that she is pregnant. She has a dream in which she wakes in her parents' house, falling out of bed, to find that it has been sold.

She is now painting things that are not actually there in front of her such as clothes wringers. She knows these objects must be memories though she cannot identify them. They are suffused with anxiety. She paints three sofas, one apple-green, with an egg-cup and broken shell, five times life size; she paints a bouquet of deadly nightshade in a glass jar, with cat's eyes dimly visible among a tangle of leaves (p. 337).

The repressed experiences of her childhood are now returning. While this goes on in her own imaginative life, Elaine watches Jon with detachment. He notices nothing. She feels completely unreal (p. 388) and begins to bite her nails again. Suddenly she paints Mrs Smeath, who floats up without warning. She feels the old anxiety: 'Whatever has happened to me is my own fault' (p. 338). Pictures of Mrs Smeath now begin to multiply.

NOTES AND GLOSSARY:

commercial illustrations: that is, Pop Art in the manner pioneered by Andy Warhol (1928–87), with his Campbell's Soup Can series in the 1960s

draft-dodgers: young Americans avoiding conscription ('being drafted') during the Vietnam War

limbo: no place (originally a place that is neither heaven nor hell, reserved for the souls of the unbaptised)

drugstore: chemist (or pharmacy)

Chapter 61

Elaine is living with Jon in a semi-detached house; she is twenty-eight and it is the 1960s. They got married in the City Hall because she was pregnant, but did not go to Niagara Falls for their honeymoon. Her daughter Sarah is two. During her first year, Elaine was 'fogged by hormones' (p. 340). Now she is coming out of it, but she still paints little for want of confidence.

Jon plays hide-and-seek with Sarah, hiding from Elaine, and this annoys Elaine. Her love for him is physical and wordless: he glows for her and she feels he is hers, but he is unable to remain faithful (p. 341). Fights begin and she stores up resentment. Jon wants enthusiasm for himself and his ideas, not capitulation. Now he is working in a graphics studio, producing motorised objects with monster-movie eyes (p. 342). He is often absent from home.

Elaine attends women's meetings, but she feels nervous at them, finding the idea of sisterhood more difficult than brotherhood. At night she paints a picture called *Our Lady of Perpetual Help* in which the Virgin Mary is wild-looking and fierce (p. 345). Jon wants her to give up painting: her work is irrelevant, marginal, as if the twentieth century had never happened. Their fights become more frequent and they start throwing things at one another.

NOTES AND GLOSSARY:

honeymoon: vacation for newly-weds

Niagara Falls: on the border between America and Canada, a popular honeymoon spot for Americans in the period. Jon was born there

nuclear families: conventional (non-extended) two-parent families, named after the nucleus of atoms

histrionics: stagey or melodramatic behaviour (unconnected with 'hysteria')

Chapter 62

Carolyn, Jody, Zillah, and Elaine, the artists in the women's group, plan a joint exhibition to be held in a defunct supermarket. Jody, who writes the programme, misinterprets the feelings behind Elaine's paintings of Mrs Smeath, which she sees as compassion for the ageing female body (p. 348). At the preview Elaine has misgivings about her work: she feels that she is marginal; the other artists have more close women-friends than she has.

At the exhibition Elaine senses Mrs Smeath's eyes watching her from the paintings. It is still a mystery to her why she should hate Mrs Smeath so much. Suddenly a woman who looks very much like Mrs Smeath enters the gallery and loudly accuses her of blasphemy. She throws a bottle of ink at *White Gift*, which shows Mrs Smeath with the heart of a dying turtle and the stencilled words 'THE KINGDOM OF GOD IS WITHIN YOU' underneath. This causes a newspaper sensation, and so makes the show a popular success: 'Some dimension of heroism has been added to me', Elaine reflects (p. 354).

NOTES AND GLOSSARY:
turtle: see Chapter 32
THE KINGDOM . . . : see Chapter 18

Chapter 63

Elaine goes to visit Cordelia at the Dorothy Lyndwick Rest Home, an up-market 'funny-farm' (p. 355). Cordelia is being given tranquillizers to sedate her; she attempted suicide because things were going badly for her (p. 358). Elaine takes her out to a nearby café. Cordelia asks Elaine to take her home with her. Elaine cannot see this working with the baby, or with Jon; besides, she is not feeling totally 'glued together' (p. 359) either. She finds herself seething with a fury that cannot be explained merely as anger at the ill-judged request. Cordelia says that Elaine has always hated her, and she denies it; she cannot remember ever having hated Cordelia.

Later Elaine dreams of Cordelia looking like a 'snow angel', falling through the air (p. 360). Some time after that, she writes to Cordelia but gets no reply. This fills her with apprehension: Cordelia is out there somewhere, about to turn up at her door. She dreams of a statue with Cordelia's head in a white cloth beneath its arm.

NOTES AND GLOSSARY:
funny-farms: (*slang*) mental asylums
tranquillizers: sedatives

XII: One Wing

The painting of this title commemorates the death of Risley's brother Stephen. In it he is shown falling 'faster than the speed of light' (p. 391) to his death; he is wearing a flier's uniform and carries a wooden sword (p. 407). The title is inspired by a song about returning air-pilots which the children learnt during the war (p. 24) (the subject of an acknowledgement of copyright at the start of the novel). When Elaine first hears the song it strikes her as sad, but here it epitomises Stephen's boyish adventurousness of spirit and his vulnerability. For Charna, the painting is merely a comment on the 'juvenile nature of war' (p. 407).

Chapter 64
Risley goes into the 4-D's Diner, a brand new version of the café typical of the American 1940s, just like Sunnysides where she and Cordelia used to sit (p. 363). She drinks some coffee, listening to the young people's enthusiasm for the setting, and reflects that the past is only quaint at a distance (p. 363). The waitress is uninterested to know that she was familiar with the original. When a zucchini in the shape of Elvis Presley's head catches Risley's attention, she imagines the discarded artefacts of the past all lining up 'waiting their turn for re-entry' (p. 364).

Around the corner she comes upon Josef's former neighbourhood again. He must be sixty-five by now: if he was a 'dirty old man' (p. 364) then, she wonders, what must he be like now? She thinks she once saw a film that he made. In it two women entangled with the same man were acting violently towards themselves or others. The director obviously thought that women cannot have their own reasons for unhappiness. All the same she thinks she was unfair to him; but she concludes that young women need unfairness to protect themselves (p. 365). Her thoughts turn to *Life Drawing*, a painting in which Josef and Jon feature: both naked, they paint a model, also naked. Each interprets her according to his own idea of woman. The model face is a sphere of glass like the cat's eye marble (p. 366).

Risley meets Jon at Park Plaza Roof Bar where she dined formerly with Josef. They drink white wine spritzers and say little, though she touches his fingers. Afterwards they return to his apartment where they make love (p. 367). Risley does not feel disloyal to her husband Ben: this is something from before his time that does not concern him (p. 368). She gently assesses Jon's physical condition and her own, now altered by age, and reflects that they have done this 'just in time' (p. 368).

NOTES AND GLOSSARY:

diner: restaurant with a bar counter and booths, common in small-town North America

frump:	(*slang*) unattractive woman
booby-trap:	usually hidden explosives set to be triggered by the victim
pre-Raphaelite:	an aesthetic movement associated with the painter Gabriel Dante Rossetti (1828–82) and others
spritzers:	white wine mixed with mineral water, a fashionable drink in the 1980s
Elvis Presley:	(1935–77) the 'King' of Rock and Roll music
zucchini:	small vegetable marrows; courgettes
dirty old man:	cant expression for an older man with an unseemly interest in young women
Regency:	early nineteenth-century period characterised by slender furniture and swagged curtains

Chapter 65

Elaine's marriage continues to deteriorate; Jon is away more, and often when she returns she finds tell-tale signs of infidelity (p. 371). A woman called Monica rings but he makes light of it. Elaine is storing these things up for when she needs them. Life goes on, though the atmosphere is heavy with unspoken accusations (p. 370).

One afternoon Jon accuses her of having had an affair with Hrbik. Soon he wants to know who else there has been (p. 371). When she counter-charges him with his infidelities, he claims credit for openness in comparison with her hypocritical pretence of purity. She retorts that she has no time for love affairs: she has to earn the rent for both of them. Now she has gone too far. Jon leaves to see Trisha – Monica was 'just a friend' (p. 371).

Elaine is sick with colds throughout the winter. She does not paint and does not respond to calls from Jody. During this period she is self-accusing (p. 372). One night when Jon does not return, Elaine hears the same inner voice she heard urging her to jump off the bridge in childhood: Cordelia's voice at the age of nine. It says, '*Do it. Come on. Do it.*' (p. 373). Elaine cuts her wrist with an Exacto knife but Jon arrives in time to take her to the hospital. She passes the cut off with the medical staff as an accident.

NOTES AND GLOSSARY:

Exacto knife:	brand-name hobby knife with sharp, replaceable blade
a shrink:	(*slang*) psychiatrist (from 'head-shrinker')

Chapter 66

Elaine is afraid that the voice will return; if she commits suicide Sarah will be motherless. One morning she draws her money from the bank and packs her cases. Jon arrives just before she goes; he only says that he cannot stop her (p. 376). This strikes her as true. She leaves with Sarah and takes the train to Vancouver. There she rents a house and finds a school for Sarah, living off her grant money, and soon gets work refinishing for an antique dealer. She starts going to a psychiatrist, but he only wants to hear about her life up to the age of six and about her orgasms. She becomes involved with a women's group, but cannot share their enthusiasm or their lesbianism (p. 379).

Contact with her parents and with Stephen is limited to postcards and presents for Sarah. When she becomes depressed she lies down and lets the wave of blackness wash over her (p. 380). She suddenly finds herself at the front of a small wave of fashion in the Vancouver art world, where her reputation has preceded her, and her pictures begin to sell for good prices.

She has unsatisfactory affairs with men at intervals, breaking off before they reject her. She meets Ben, a divorced man ten years her senior, in a supermarket; he would have been too dull and simple-minded for her before, but she enjoys mundane happiness with him. They travel to Mexico, then they get married. To her this is a defiance of convention, but not to him (p. 381). They have a daughter, Anne.

Ben thinks of her as 'good' (p. 381); he runs the business side of her career. He does not understand her paintings but admires the skill with which she does hands. Toronto is still at a great distance and she dares not look at it, like the biblical Gomorrah.

NOTES AND GLOSSARY:

toytown:	a derogatory term for modern suburbs, which look like children's building sets
Gomorrah:	one of the cities of the plain destroyed by God in Genesis 18–19. Lot's wife looked back and was turned into a pillar of salt

XIII: Picoseconds

The painting of this name shows a landscape with a remote view of Risley's parents picnicking (p. 405). There are petrol pump logos beneath. *Picoseconds* connotes the first moments of the universe as described in Stephen's lecture (p. 331), but here it alludes to the beginnings of family life for Elaine Risley. She compares it with Breugel's *Fall of Icarus* (p. 405) in which the drowning young man makes no more than a small splash on the canvas, indicating that the universe is indifferent to individual suffering (as W. H. Auden suggested in a famous poem). Although neither Icarus nor Stephen are in this painting, they both died more or less the same way. That parallel makes his death seem pre-ordained, and parents seem pregnant with his death as much as with his life in this picture.

TO42390

Chapter 67

Risley wakes up the morning after sleeping with Jon. She feels that she has dispensed a dismissal and a blessing, like medieval saints with their hand upraised (p. 385). She eats an egg in a cup (the way they were eaten at home before Cordelia arrived in Toronto). She is killing time: the hours before the opening will be like a textureless interlude.

She goes walking in the cemetery, looking for silver paper and such things, as she did in childhood (p. 385). She passes the lawn where Cordelia made the snow angel. It is All Souls' Eve and there are pumpkins on the porches, and she can taste the children's festival. Risley reflects how differently this is done in Mexico: unlike them we like to make the dead unmentionable, therefore our dead are harder to hear and hungrier.

NOTES AND GLOSSARY:

interlude: theatrical term for short performance in the middle of the main event

bag lady: a destitute woman who carries her possessions through the streets in shopping bags

pumpkins: in North American at Hallowe'en pumpkins are hollowed out as 'heads' with candles burning inside

All Souls' Eve: Hallowe'en (so named in Chapter 20)

Chapter 68

Risley narrates the death of her brother Stephen five years previously, reconstructing events from the scant information given her. The flight he is taking to Frankfurt, where he was to give a paper, has been high-jacked by Arab terrorists. The women and children on board have been released. Stephen hopes the gunmen will keep their heads and that none of the passengers will go crazy. One of the men orders him to get up from his seat and he is led to a door which is then opened. Stephen is pushed out; Risley reflects that this was the way in which her brother entered the past (p. 391).

She concludes that Stephen died of an eye for an eye, 'or someone's idea of it' (p. 388). When she goes to identify the body, she thinks about his theory of the space twin: now she will get older and he will not (p. 392).

NOTES AND GLOSSARY:

an eye for an eye: a celebrated definition of justice (see the Bible, Book of Exodus (21:24). It was revised by Jesus in the Sermon of the Mount (see Matthew 5:38–39))

changes when you look at it: according to Heisenberg's uncertainty principle, scientific observation alters the state of the

	thing observed. Stephen Hawking deals with this in *A Brief History of Time* (1988), Chapter 4
Frankfurt:	German city
adrenalin:	(adrenaline) hormone released in response to danger and excitement
berserk:	crazy, wild; originally the violence of marauding Vikings
speed of light:	186,000 miles per second. Stephen is travelling faster than light because he is travelling into the past, which is outside of 'time'

Chapter 69
Stephen's parents do not recover from the death of their son. Elaine's father dies suddenly; her mother contracts a painful disease and is thankful that her husband went quickly (p. 393).

One day she starts to talk about the time that Elaine nearly froze: it was during the period when those girls gave her 'a bad time' (p. 394). Elaine is unwilling to think about Cordelia whom she feels she has been neglecting. Her mother tells her that the girls said Elaine had been kept in at school, but she had not believed them. She thinks that Carol Campbell was to blame because Cordelia was Elaine's best friend later on in high school (p. 395).

Unpacking the steamer trunk together, mother and daughter unearth mementoes of Elaine's childhood such as Stephen's drawings and report cards and her scrapbooks and photograph album, but also a red purse containing the blue cat's eye marble. When Elaine looks into it, all the repressed events return to her consciousness. She sees her entire life (p. 398) in a glass sphere of the cat's eye.

NOTES AND GLOSSARY:
sepia-coloured: the brownish colour of fading photographs

Chapter 70
Risley walks in the vicinity of the store where they bought sweets at school. She moves on expecting to see the primary school with its BOYS and GIRLS doors, but the building has disappeared. For a moment she feels physically stricken by this absence, as if winded. The new school nearby is unsegregated (p. 400). It looks as if there can be no cruelty here, no secrets. She reaches the wooden steps that lead up the hill and feels a malevolent ill-will surrounding her. She pleads with Cordelia inwardly: she does not want to be nine-years-old forever.

NOTES AND GLOSSARY:
store: American usage for 'shop'

Georgius VI . . .:   the Latin inscription on the British coins of the period
regalia: clothing and adornments of kings and queens, the symbols of their royalty

---

XIV: Unified Field Theory

Perhaps surprisingly the painting of this name – taken from Stephen's physics lecture (p. 331) – has a religious subject. It shows the Virgin of Lost Things in black on the bridge where the Virgin Mary who 'rescued' Elaine stood. The Virgin holds 'an oversized blue cat's eye marble' (p. 408) near her heart. Under the bridge are stars but also a dark tangle that represents 'the underside of the ground' (p. 408). At the lower edge is the 'land of the dead people' (p. 408) representing the graveyard that lies nearby. The most significant thing about the painting is, perhaps, that it is a bridge, suggesting that it shares a subject (and associations) with the next part and its title.

Chapter 71
Risley dresses for the opening, putting on the black dress she bought after all. Reaching the gallery early, she finds that paintings have been arranged in chronological order: first still lives, then Josef and Jon; then the many pictures of Mrs Smeath. She realises now that Mrs Smeath's eyes are 'self-righteous . . . piggy and smug' (p. 405), but also melancholy and uncertain and 'heavy with unloved duty' (p. 405). Risley feels that she has done her an injustice in the paintings. She believes now that 'an eye for an eye' can only lead to more blindness (p. 405).

Among the new paintings are *Picoseconds*, showing her parents making a picnic; *Three Muses*, framing Mrs Finestein, Mr Banerji and Miss Stuart; and *One Wing*, painted for Stephen. The fourth, *Cat's Eye*, is a partial self-portrait in a mirror with three girls in the background. The final picture, called *Unified Field Theory*, shows the Virgin of Lost Things floating above the railings of the wooden bridge.

Risley thought she was preserving something from time when she painted all these pictures (p. 409). She knows this is impossible in real time, which is a blur, a 'moving edge' (p. 409). She is momentarily tempted to burn them all, yet recognises that they have now taken on independent life and meaning: she is the remnant (p. 409).

NOTES AND GLOSSARY:
mimeo machine: brand-name for a portable printing system using wax stencils taken from a typewriter
symbiosis: growing together (biological term)
jeu d'esprit: light-hearted work of art (literally 'a game of the spirit' in French)

Group of Seven:	members of a Canadian art movement
postmodern:	(usually 'post-modern') pertaining to the intellectual movement after modernism that treats styles as arbitrary
pastiche:	a work of art that imitates another work or works, often combining such borrowed materials or styles
Breugel:	Pieter Breugel (?1525–69); his *Fall of Icarus* shows a youth with man-made wings plunging to his death in the sea
Studebaker:	American make of car
frescoes:	paintings done on wet plaster
logos:	insignias of companies or corporations
Muses:	the muses are the immortals who inspire the arts in Greek mythology
numinous:	having to do with a deity or presiding spirit (Latin *numen*)
Jan Gossaert:	(*d.c.* 1533) a Dutch painter noted for an overabundance of detail which art historians attribute to *horror vacui* ('fear of emptiness')

Chapter 72
Charna takes Risley into an inner room until the opening gets going, and then proudly brings her out to meet the guests (p. 411). Risley expects to see people who knew her when she lived in Toronto, but most of all she is looking for Cordelia. She no longer needs to ask what happened during the time she lost; instead she needs to know Cordelia's accounts of why it happened. Cordelia too needs Elaine's version to give her back a part of herself: the two are like the twins in old fables who each have half a key. But Cordelia does not appear.

An enthusiastic young woman artist whom Risley recognises as 'post everything' (p. 412) comes and tells her how much she loves *Falling Women*. Risley feels institutionalised by such comments but manages to thank her. After the show she turns down Charna's invitation to further celebrations and goes home exhausted (p. 413). She was prepared for anything except the absence of Cordelia.

NOTES AND GLOSSARY:

post everything:	the prefix 'post-' is used to indicate versions of conceptual outlooks such as 'modernism', 'structuralism', 'feminism', and so on, in which their status as cultural 'constructs' is acknowledged and developed as 'methodologies' rather than literal theories
gangrene:	decay of flesh on a living body which spreads and causes death by poison

Chapter 73

Back in the studio apartment, she thinks of Cordelia: *'You're dead'*. But the Cordelia who inhabits her refuses to lie down.

NOTES AND GLOSSARY:
You're dead ... Lie down: phrases used by children playing games involving shooting

---

XV: Bridge

No painting of this name is described in the novel, but it is likely that Risley painted one since she had a dream in which she found herself on a bridge that became detached at either end (p. 145). Her mother was talking to people at the side and did not notice her predicament (p. 145). It is possible that this refers, however, to the painting called *Unified Field Theory* under a simpler name.

Chapter 74

Risley sleeps until noon on the following day and misses her plane. She takes a walk from the demolished school to the bridge itself, which she finally intends to visit. In the ravine, now a joggers' pathway, the deadly nightshade plants have been cleared away, but she knows that Stephen's jar of marbles is still down there (p. 418). Over the parapet she can see the bank of the stream on which she was standing when she heard the voice of the Virgin Mary. All of these memories have come back to her with absolute clarity, but now she can appreciate that there was no voice, no lady in a dark cloak and no red heart (p. 418).

She hears the sound of someone approaching and, thinking it is Cordelia, she feels the shame she felt when she was in the power of this child at nine. She knows that these are not her own emotions; they always belonged to Cordelia. Elaine is now the stronger, and the other will freeze to death if she stays behind. Elaine extends a hand. In her mind she tells Cordelia that she can go home now, using the very words spoken to her by the Virgin Mary all those years ago (p. 419).

When she turns it is not Cordelia but a middle-aged woman with a dog. There is nothing but the bridge, the river and the sky as they are when Elaine Risley is not there. This landscape is 'filled with whatever it is by itself' (p. 419) when she is absent.

NOTES AND GLOSSARY:
go home: see Chapter 35

Chapter 75

On the flight to Vancouver, Elaine Risley finds herself beside two ladies making the most of their old age (p. 420). Elaine addresses Cordelia inwardly, summing up her remaining sense of loss. It is not so much something that is gone, but something that can never happen: two old women laughing together (p. 421).

As you look out of the plane the night sky is clear and full of stars, remote echoes of something that happened millions of years ago. It is 'old light, and there's not much of it' (p. 421), but 'it's enough to see by' (p. 421).

NOTES AND GLOSSARY:

Echoes of light: see Stephen's account of the stars in Chapter 19 (pp. 104–5)

shining out of the midst of nothing: compare 'And the light shineth in darkness; and the darkness comprehended it not' (see the Bible, John 1:5). 'Comprehended' here means 'enclose and smother'

Part 3

Commentary

Structure

The text

The novel *Cat's Eye* is narrated by a painter (Elaine Risley) who tells the story of her life up to the present moment as it has shaped her personality and her art. What she recounts mostly concerns the history of a young girl bullied by other children with lasting emotional effects. In the course of her narrative she also recounts the stages by which she recovered repressed memories of that experience through painting, up to the time when she meets with the cat's eye marble which finally brings them back to her in their entirety. Now she has come to Toronto to open a retrospective exhibition of those paintings in which her story is embodied in images and symbols (though only the narrator and the reader know this about them). In other words, *Cat's Eye* is both a psychoanalytical novel and a bildungsroman.* Since it incorporates many concepts from the world of modern physics as well as from other areas of contemporary intellectual culture, it is also a novel of ideas. Finally, since it 'deconstructs' many features of the decades in which it is set, holding them up for inspection as specific social and cultural formations, it can also be called a post-modernist novel, even though the narrator herself disparages the term 'post-modern'.

Cat's Eye is an autobiographical novel in the sense that the central character conducts her own narrative (the technical term for this is 'autodiegesis'); however, she does not literally 'write' that narrative; indeed, she is a painter not a writer. It may be best, then, to think of the novel as a monologue spoken in conversation with a listener or listeners who can be trusted to understand her viewpoint, her thematic interests, her ironic comments and her self-effacing jokes. This 'audience' is, however, no less an invention than the story she is telling. As the narrator in another

---

*A bildungsroman (from the German word meaning 'novel of growth') is a novel that describes the development of an artist. In English the best-known examples are *Sons and Lovers* (1913) by D. H. Lawrence and *A Portrait of the Artist as a Young Man* (1916) by James Joyce. Another classic, Marcel Proust's *A la recherche du temps perdu* (1913–22); translated by C. K. Scott Moncrieff as *Remembrance of Things Past*, 1922–31) shares a feature with *Cat's Eye*: in that novel a piece of madeleine cake brings the whole past back to mind for the central character, just as the cat's eye brings Elaine Risley's entire life before her mind (p. 398).

Atwood novel says, 'By telling you anything at all I'm at least believing in you, I believe you're there, I believe you into being . . . I tell, therefore you are' (*The Handmaid's Tale*, 1987, p. 279).

Whether the narrator is describing the present moment or events of long ago, the narrative is conducted in the present tense (or 'historic present'), a technique often used in informal story-telling. As a literary device, this creates the impression that past and present are part of a simultaneous order of existence – an idea advanced at the beginning of the novel where she describes the different phases of her life as a series of 'liquid transparencies' (p. 3). In keeping with this view, the narrative largely consists of a series of flashbacks in which the narrator, now in early middle age, reconstructs episodes of her childhood and early womanhood, returning by chronological stages to the present moment. Interspersed with these extended re-creations of the past, however, are shorter passages dealing with her experiences in the present.

The novel is divided into fifteen major parts (I–XV), each of which takes its name from one of Risley's paintings gathered for the exhibition. The seventy-five chapters of the book are numbered continuously without regard to these major divisions. Within each chapter there is also a variable number of sub-sections. There is an approximate symmetry in the design of each titled part (roughly averaging five chapters in scope). Generally the opening chapters deal with events in Toronto during the three days of Elaine's visit, as she goes to and from the gallery, to restaurants, or to other places she remembers. After that, the narrative takes up the chronology of events in the narrator's earlier life, advancing from childhood to adolescence, onwards to young womanhood, and finally to maturity when she 'becomes' the narrator herself.

This design allows for a great deal of refraction between the different sections of the narrative and it is organised throughout with a studied awareness of how the language in every passage chimes with that in all the others. Symbols (which are chiefly connected with the paintings) and phrases that recur time after time measure the persistence or alteration of ideas in the central character's mind. Many of these also reveal the novelist's concern about the conditions of existence, particularly the difficulty of knowing anything certain about it. Though Margaret Atwood's use of drifting symbolism increases the impression that the meaning of life is uncertain, hard to excavate, and so, it follows, risky to define, there is nevertheless a clear sense that a definite set of values and beliefs is affirmed in the novel.

For some critics this novel (as well as others by Margaret Atwood) is not only post-modernist but also post-feminist. It involves a feminine way of writing (*écriture féminine*) that 'perceives the world in terms of ambiguities, pluralities, processes, continuities and complex relationships', as distinct from 'patriarchal expressive modes' that see the world 'in terms of categories, dichotomies, roles, stasis and causation'.* Since the narrator herself expresses considerable disaffection from feminist cliques and, more generally, the post-modernism 'dogmas' (p. 379) on which such criticism is founded, it would be dangerous to ascribe such motives to the novelist. In fact, her writing participates in both methods of composition – if the distinction is valid at all. There are both ambiguities and dichotomies in its way of mapping (or unmapping) the world we live in.

The paintings

The title of each part in *Cat's Eye* is taken from a painting by Risley – as is the title of the novel. Two exceptions, however, are the first and last parts ('Iron Lung' and 'Bridge'), for which there are no corresponding paintings. The connection between the titles of successive parts and the corresponding painting is not always easy to fathom. In some cases it is obvious: 'Empire Bloomers' narrates details about the off-putting undergarments worn by Miss Lumley, the schoolroom authoritarian who first teaches Elaine. 'Cat's Eye', however, makes no reference to the cat's eye marble or even to cats' eyes, though it is the chapter in which Elaine learns to imitate the way in which the marble appears to 'see' things without feeling any pain (p. 173). Given such differences, it seems most likely that the order of titles in the novel follows the chronology established in the exhibition catalogue as arranged by Charna (p. 404), and therefore roughly corresponds to the order of events in Elaine Risley's life as they are reflected in her paintings.

Most of the pictures give allegorical accounts of their subjects which can only be read correctly in the light of the biographical information provided in the narrative. Risley's critics, who lack this information, are comically inaccurate in their accounts of them – a circumstance based on the fact that she has only herself discovered the rationale of her painting a very few years before and (presumably) has not cared to disclose it to the ravenous art world. Up to her encounter with the cat's eye marble, it is solely through the paintings that Elaine can bring back to consciousness the hidden episodes of her childhood, and several of the subjects seem like 'archetypes' unearthed in this way.

The approximate moment in the narrative when Elaine encountered the cat's eye in her mother's house can be determined from the date of Stephen's death five years prior to the time of narration (p. 388); in the interim Elaine's father has died (p. 393), and her mother has grown older;

*Julia Penelope and Susan J. Wolfe, 'Consciousness as style: style as aesthetic', in Barrie Thorne, *et al.* (eds), *Language, Gender and Society*, Massachusetts, 1983; quoted in Marion Lomax, 'Gendered Writing and the Writer's Stylistic Identity', in Katie Wales (ed.), *Feminist Linguistics in Literary Cricism, Essays and Studies* (for the English Association; Gen. ed. D. S. Brewer), 1994, pp. 1–19.

some time after the discovery of the marble her mother dies also (p. 393). That makes the moment of recovered memory not more than three and possibly less than two years before the retrospective exhibition. Obviously some of the paintings were done long before that incident; others follow after. In fact the character of her painting differs widely depending on whether they are done before or after that event. Those which precede it reflect the emergence of partial memories from her unconscious as unrecognised objects charged with the anxiety of her original trauma surface in the paintings. Those which come after are more tranquil reconstructions of memories of the past, composed in the light of a more complete understanding of the people and events reflected in them.

For instance, the Mrs Smeath paintings (such as *White Gift* and *Leprosy*) appeared in the joint exhibition in Toronto fifteen or twenty years earlier (p. 350). Others such as *One Wing* and *Picoseconds* are designated 'new paintings' (p. 405) in the current catalogue. These show a much fuller and more reflective awareness of the circumstances of her childhood whereas the earlier 'archetypal' sofas, wringers and toasters merely welled up unbidden from her troubled unconscious. The new pictures, then, represent a final understanding of her psychological history, and therefore 'read' the same way as the later chapters of the novel. In this way the painting called *Unified Field Theory* represents a coming-to-terms with the forces that enslaved Elaine in her childhood in a way that *Deadly Nightshade* does not and cannot do since it contains things such as the cats' eyes that she did not understand even as she painted them (p. 337), and which – unsurprisingly – others failed to understand as well (p. 351).

The descriptions of the paintings are so convincing that they survive long after in the reader's memory and can easily be imagined as actually existing and forming the inspiration of the novel. It is therefore worth emphasising that no such paintings as these actually exist and that they are essentially literary – rather than artistic – creations, as the author's note on the back of the title-page emphatically insists. It is obvious that Atwood must have invented the plot before she could decide which episodes to encapsulate as paintings, and this implies a period of design and adaptation that is well worth thinking about if one is to understand the structure of the resultant novel. The post-structuralist term 'bricolage' seems to apply (used to mean making a work of art out of bits and pieces). Risley laid her materials on the drawing-board and worked out how they would fit together before she did any of the real writing.

There is no better example of the advance thinking that went on than the aesthetic make-up of the central character. Elaine Risley has been given a definite view of her art. In adopting the egg tempera method of painting associated with the early Renaissance (p. 326) and chiefly used for religious murals, she turns her back not only on the whole tradition of oil-painting but also on the abstract style and acrylic paints so often used by modern painters. Atwood makes her a 'post-modernist' painter in a very individual sense: she has abandoned modernism for older techniques and more individual sources of inspiration that refuse to be mistaken for *avant garde*. In addition, she has a highly individual and intensely imaginative vocabulary of images based on irreducibly personal experience (the substance of the novel). In this way the Risley paintings strongly affirm the 'selfhood' of the artist. Nevertheless – and this is a point with far-reaching implications – Elaine Risley is an imagined artist, not a real one. Perhaps selfhood itself is always imaginary.

Characters

Elaine Risley

The middle-aged narrator is a painter (not an 'artist' (pp. 15; 89)). She was brought up in Toronto but now lives in Vancouver with her second husband in a marriage which is comfortable but not passionate. She is still prone to depressions on account of the period of bullying that she underwent at the age of nine, and was reluctant to return to Toronto for the opening of her retrospective exhibition for that reason.

She dresses in comfortable clothes, never aims to be in fashion (p. 87), and prefers domestic disorder to staying in hotels. She is fearful of her growing eminence as an artist and hates to feel that she is turning into an institution (pp. 226; 412). During adolescence she developed what she calls 'a mean mouth' (p. 234) and can still make stinging remarks. She says many witty and sardonic things about the world around her in Toronto and the people she has known there. She believes herself to be 'vengeful, greedy, secretive and sly' (p. 153), but the reader also recognises her compassion and her concern with justice and her indignation at political oppression (p. 403).

Risley has a searching, sceptical mind and takes a no-nonsense view of life informed by left-wing views of history and society. She is agnostic in religion and dislikes parties and dogmas of all kinds; she distrusts groups who do their thinking collectively or permit it to be done for them (pp. 90; 379). She is contemptuous of intellectual trends and particularly dislikes the jargon of art criticism (pp. 89; 226). A humanist who has measured the difficulty of constructing an existence without ideology or creed, she has emerged with a tenuous belief in the possibility of understanding self and others.

Stephen

Elaine's brother is highly intelligent. As a boy he plays inventively and is given to collecting things, which he does with great thoroughness. He wins a scholarship to a private school and devotes himself from an early age to 'The Nature of the Universe' (p. 290), moving away rapidly from 'the imprecision of words' (p. 3) into post-Euclidean mathematics. He is contemptuous of boys who are fixated on girls (p. 221) and dresses untidily (p. 331).

Stephen is kind to Elaine when they are children together, teaching her to play his games and sharing secrets with her (p. 25). Despite the difference in their ages, she believes that he made the best of her (p. 333). As a young scientist Stephen transmits to Elaine the conception of universe as a space–time continuum that informs the novel (p. 219). His death is commemorated in the painting *One Wing* (p. 407), which shows him falling from an airplane with a wooden sword in his hand just like the ones he made in childhood. This suggests that in spite of his scientific intelligence he never really grew up emotionally, as his sister Elaine did.

Elaine's father

An entomologist in the Zoology department in the university of Toronto, he is a kindly, intelligent man who makes dire predictions about the fate of the human species in the belief that we have neglected the basic lessons of science about the environment (p. 248). He will not have a television in the house because it rots the brain and gives out subliminal messages. He dislikes industrial society and regards 'Rudolph the Red-nosed Reindeer' as a 'nauseating commercial neologism' (p. 128). He is a liberal and an atheist.

> My father says he doesn't believe in brainwashing children. When you're grown up, then you can make up your own mind about religion, which has been responsible for a lot of wars and massacres in his opinion, as well as bigotry and intolerance (p. 96).

Elaine's mother

She is not interested in housework or household furnishings and wears what is most comfortable, showing 'irreverent carelessness' (p. 214) towards fashion. She 'doesn't give a hoot' (p. 214) about what people think. Like her husband she is kindly and liberal in her outlook. She does not attempt to dominate her children, but neither does she know what to do when Elaine is being victimised by the other girls. Risley later thinks that her mother's cheerfulness has always been 'profoundly willed' (p. 396). Her first name is not given in any part of the novel.

Carol Campbell

The first girl Elaine meets at school is Carol, a short girl who laughs frequently (p. 47) and finds Elaine's family home ridiculous because it does not have the latest fashions and appliances (p. 49). She is an obsequious accomplice of Cordelia's when the latter is bullying Elaine, but occasionally she herself becomes the victim instead (p. 121). The first of the girls to develop breasts, she later takes to running in a provocative way to attract boys (p. 202).

> Carol cries too easily and noisily, she gets carried away with her own crying. She draws attention, she can't be depended on not to tell. There's a recklessness in her, she can be pushed just so far, she has a weak sense of honour, she's reliable only as an informer (p. 121)

Carol's mother

Mrs Campbell has put chintz on the windows; she wears a twin set and has her hair done in a cold wave. She and her husband don't sleep together; rather they have identical twin beds. She has a turned-down mouth even when she is smiling (p. 51).

Grace Smeath

Grace is a year older than the others. Elaine and Carol compete for her friendship until Cordelia comes along. The girls play at her house, which is furnished out of Eaton's catalogue. She gets headaches if she is told what to do (p. 52). The girls put up with her because they to want to play with her (p. 52). Elaine's mother believes that Grace was behind the bullying of Elaine, but Grace lacks the conviction to operate the more subtle forms of torment (p. 171). She still believes that babies are made by God (p. 94).

Mrs Smeath

Like her sister Mabel (who was formerly a missionary in China), Grace's mother is an evangelical Protestant. A big-boned woman, with gapped, square teeth and raw-looking skin, she parts her hair severely in the middle (p. 57). Her bibbed aprons make it seem as if she has only one breast stretching down to her waist (p. 57). She is said to have a bad heart and spends a lot of time lying on a sofa (p. 57).

Mrs Smeath brings Elaine to church with the family and teaches her to feel ashamed of her own non-church parents. She regards Elaine's persecution by Cordelia and the other girls as 'God's punishment' (p. 180). The injustice of this view makes her a hate-object in many of the Risley paintings of the 'Empire Bloomers' series. It takes Elaine many years to remember why she hates her so much (p. 58), and finally to forgive her (p. 405).

It's the eyes I look at now. I used to think these were self-righteous eyes, piggy and smug inside their wire frames; and they are. But they are also defeated eyes . . . The eyes of someone for whom God was a sadistic old man; the eyes of a threadbare small-town decency. Mrs Smeath was a transplant to the city, from somewhere a lot smaller (p. 405).

Mr Smeath

Mr Smeath is a short, flabby man (p. 126) who participates in the family's religious observations on Sundays although clearly more interested in train-spotting (p. 164). He cracks irreverent jokes at the dinner-table, calling beans the 'musical fruit' that makes people 'toot' (p. 126). Elaine experiences embarrassment when he enlists her support for his vulgar good humour although she does not know that 'toot' means 'fart'.

Cordelia

Cordelia arrives in the neighbourhood after the other girls, but immediately takes control of the gang. She has a lop-sided mouth, grey-green eyes, and wears a closed, defiant expression (p. 419). Her parents have named her after the good daughter in Shakespeare's *King Lear* (p. 263).

Cordelia impresses Elaine's parents with her good manners, but has a poor relationship with her own father: nothing she can do will please him (p. 249). The feelings of guilt occasioned by this rejection are redirected at Elaine. Although she abuses Elaine psychologically and makes Carol and Grace torment her, she never actually hurts her physically. She persuades Elaine that the punishments she imposes on her are for her own good.

As she grows older Cordelia begins to fail at school and starts shoplifting for fun (p. 210). Elaine triumphs over her during their teenage years by frightening her with talk about vampires (pp. 232–3). Elaine comes to believe that she and Cordelia have 'changed places' (p. 227). On graduating from high school Cordelia spends some time in a mental hospital following a suicide attempt (p. 358). Elaine refuses to help her escape and loses touch with her soon after, but it is Cordelia's nine-year-old voice that later prompts her to attempt to commit suicide (p. 373).

Towards the end of the novel, Risley thinks that she and Cordelia are like twins in a fairy tale each of whom has been given half a key, and she is determined to give back to Cordelia her own reflection (p. 411), the emotions which are rightly Cordelia's and always have been (p. 419).

Cordelia's father

A successful businessman with good looks, a dashing smile, and great personal charm, he is the centre of attention in a family composed entirely of women (p. 164). He enjoys saying the he is 'hag-ridden' (p. 249). He does not seem to like Cordelia at all and she often gets in trouble with him.

Cordelia's mother

She arranges flowers and dinners at which her husband is always treated very specially. She has three daughters. Her relationship with Cordelia is not described.

Perdie and Mirrie

Cordelia's older sisters are named after character's in Shakespearean comedies (Cordelia's name is of course tragic). Their exaggerated expressions provide the younger girls with insights into the ways of older teenagers, but also with forebodings of puberty and the world of women. They heat brown wax to remove hair from their legs and examine themselves in mirrors, making remarks about 'the curse' (p. 92). Cordelia calls them gifted, something she herself is not considered to be (p. 73).

Miss Lumley

Elaine's first teacher at Queen Mary's Public is an Empire loyalist and a classroom disciplinarian. She tells the children about the horrors of life on the dark continents before the arrival of British rule and electricity. She is believed to wear bloomers which she takes off at the back of the class. Elaine is afraid of these bloomers and sees them as a shameful secret shared equally by the girls and by Miss Lumley (p. 81).

Miss Stuart

The nicest of the teachers at Queen Mary's, Miss Stuart decorates her classroom with pictures of other people living in the empire, but unlike Miss Lumley's benighted natives these are cheerful (p. 161). She has a pronounced Scottish accent. During afternoon break she takes tea with whiskey from a silver flask (p. 154). Miss Stuart makes a brief gesture of compassion towards Elaine in her darkest hour. Risley later comes to see her as an exile from 'plundered Scotland' (p. 407).

Ben

A travel agent by profession, Risley's husband is ten years older and much more ordinary, viewing her in simpler terms than she regards herself

(p. 381). Among his sterling qualities are cheap tickets to Mexico (p. 15). He admires her pictures and says that he once wanted to paint but had to earn a living, a remark she tolerates in him as she would not in anyone else (p. 382).

Elaine met her husband in Vancouver, where they live with her daughters by Jon and by Ben. Throughout the novel she leaves affectionate messages to him on the answering phone although, in her opinion, her current encounters in Toronto simply do not concern him.

Sarah and Anne

Sarah is Elaine's daughter with Jon and Anne her daughter with Ben. They have sensible names – unlike Cordelia (p. 15). When Risley is depressed, as she sometimes is, they take it for granted that she will be all right next day; they look at everything straight and do not seem to need protection (p. 114). All the same, Elaine scans their friends for signs of hypocrisy in case they are like Cordelia (p. 118).

Jon

Elaine met her first husband at Toronto Art College where he was a student. As a young painter he captured moments of pure art process in eye-hurting colours: 'Jon is big on purity, but only in art' (p. 317). For many years he seemed to have potential, but potential does not last forever (p. 265). Latterly he makes a living from special effects for horror movies (p. 17).

When they became lovers, Jon seemed to represent for Elaine an escape from the world of grownups (p. 316). After their marriage he was frequently unfaithful, yet she now finds it easy to forgive him (p. 267), feeling towards him as towards someone with whom she has survived a traffic accident (p. 17).

Mr MacLeod

The Principal of Elaine's High School likes to think of himself as related to the Scottish titled family with which he shares a name. Unlike Miss Stuart, he does not speak with a Scottish accent and so is a Scot only by deliberate personal affiliation (p. 206). He brings the Earle Gray Players to the school for a performance of *Macbeth*, presumably because of its Scottish associations (p. 245) as well as for the syllabus requirements.

Mr Banerji

A research student, then a junior colleague of Elaine's father, Banerji is the object of prejudice in Canada. Though joined later by a wife, he can get no post at the university and he returns to India. He has the nervous laugh and haunted look of someone who never feels secure (p. 158). He is kind to Elaine, supplying her with laboratory specimens to paint.

Mrs Finestein

The Jewish next-door neighbour for whom Elaine briefly baby-sits, Mrs Finestein, dressed garishly. The other girls' racist comments force Elaine to stop working for her (p. 135). At one point Elaine dreams that she is really the child of Mr Banerji and Mrs Finestein (p. 166). When Elaine starts wearing beatnik clothes, Mrs Finestein rebukes her (p. 277). Later, Elaine wonders what 'death-camp ashes' (p. 407) blew through Mrs Finestein's mind in the years after the war.

Josef Hrbik

The Life Drawing teacher at the College of Art is in his mid-thirties, with dark curly hair, a moustache, an aquiline nose and dark eyes that seem almost purple (p. 270). The male art students are contemptuous of him (p. 281), but Elaine embarks on a sexual relationship with him in the confused belief that she is rescuing him from Susie (p. 286).

A refugee from the Hungarian Revolution, Hrbik says that his country does not exist any more and calls Elaine his 'country' in its place (p. 299). He has old-fashioned ideas about women and does not credit them with an emotional life apart from men (p. 365). Long after she has left him, Elaine acknowledges that she has no reason to blame him since they served each other's needs (p. 365).

Susie

An art student, short and heavily built (p. 281), she is in love with Hrbik and wants to marry him, but eventually becomes pregnant by him and has a disastrous abortion, calling on Elaine to take her to the hospital. Elaine, also seeing Hrbik, watches her degeneration with contempt tinged with horror since it illustrates what can happen (p. 321).

Virgin Mary

Elaine's acquaintance with this 'character' stems from a holy picture that she picks up in the street near her school (p. 182) – presumably dropped by a boy at Our Lady of Perpetual Help, the nearby Catholic school that Elaine's brother and his friends call 'Perpetual Hell' (p. 47).

When Mrs Smeath abuses Elaine she turns to the Virgin, and it is she who seems to 'rescue' her in the ravine where she nearly dies as a result of Cordelia's bullying (p. 189). Later, when that traumatic experience has been repressed, she forgets the reason why she is interested in statues of the Virgin, a taste that draws her into Catholic churches for many years, though she is always disappointed by the statues that she meets there (p. 197).

Travelling in Mexico in adult life she discovers a black Virgin of Lost Things, the first that ever seems convincing (p. 198). The Virgin appears in several of Risley's paintings including notably *Unified Field Theory* (p. 408), and Risley speaks to Cordelia in her words at the end of the novel: '*It's all right . . . You can go home now*' (p. 419). Yet Risley understands that the Virgin who rescued her was imaginary. 'There was no voice . . . Although she has come back to me now in absolute clarity . . . I know this didn't happen. There was only darkness and silence. Nobody and nothing' (p. 418).

Contexts

Canada

Canada, now a country of 24 million people, was established as a federation of provinces by an Act of British Parliament in 1867, having remained loyal to the Crown during the American War of Independence (1775–83). The original members, Nova Scotia, New Brunswick, Ontario, and Quebec (the last-named taken from the French in 1753), were joined in ensuing decades by Manitoba, British Columbia, Prince Edward Island, Alberta and Saskatchewan. Newfoundland was added after a plebiscite in 1949. Throughout the earlier period covered in this novel, Canada was a British Dominion administered by home rule under mostly Liberal governments. In April 1982 full independence ('patriation') was acknowledged by a royal visit of Elizabeth II. Canada has a dual system of parliamentary representation, provincial and national, a flexible system safe-guarded by opt-out rights for the provinces. Though French-Canadian separatism associated with the province of Quebec remains an issue, Canadians share a sense of national and cultural identity distinct from Britain on the one hand, and from America on the other. Canadian English follows British spelling and grammar but uses many American expressions. There is a Canadian accent, and (needless to say) a Canadian climate: hence the habitual references to the season at the start of so many chapters in this novel (see pp. 59, 92, 127, 140 for examples of this). In addition, the sheer scale of the empty prairie-land between the inhabited regions of Columbia and Ontario, and the vast expanse of the Northern wilderness, have had a great impact on the Canadian experience.

Cat's Eye is little concerned with the details of national politics, which it characterises with some light touches in passing only – see for instance the remarks on Canadians as Britons (p. 80). An amusing off-hand comment on the national flag adopted at independence, which Risley compares with a trademark for cheap margarine (p. 311), catches the dismissive way in which the paraphernalia of Canadian statehood are treated in the novel. Nevertheless cultural history in contemporary Canada and beyond matters greatly to her – as to the author. So much attention is given to the memorabilia of previous decades of social culture in various passages that the novel somewhat resembles an archive of information about fashions, brand-names, magazines, radio shows, popular songs, skipping songs, sayings, and the slang expressions of each decade that it covers. Toronto is more than merely a passive setting for the story. In spite of Risley's somewhat truculent disdain for the city (p. 13), the insistent use of real places such as King Street, Bloor Street, Queen Street, Harbord Street, The Annexe, and so on, suggests a love of place on the part of the narrator is spite of her profession of hatred for the city (p. 13).

Toronto today houses one of the finest collections of modern art in the world and shares fully in the fads and fashions of art and culture. Returning to find such changes, the somewhat testy narrator comments on Toronto's new trendiness (p. 19), its multiculturalism (p. 43) and its pretensions to having become a world-class city (p. 14). Risley is sceptical about that claim, believing that underneath its newly acquired European-style awnings it remains malicious, grudging and vindictive (p. 14). Further remarks in different parts of the novel provide a running commentary on Toronto. She approves of the rise of multi-ethnicity (many races), especially marked in the take-over of corner shops from the white people who used to run them (p. 151), but she has hard things to say about shopping-complexes and the consumerism they propagate and feed off (p. 111). The gentrification of run-down houses in the inner city particularly incenses her, and she pillories the interior design that goes with such bouts of urban renewal (p. 16). She notes with even greater disdain the reconstruction of the former 'Sunnysides' diner as the '4-Ds' (p. 363), and ridicules the recycling of outmoded styles epitomised by it. Again and again, she criticises the 'sawtoothed edge of trend' (p. 19) for imitating the external details of past decades without regard to the lived experience associated with them: the past is not quaint at the time, only becomes so when treated as décor (p. 363).

In another sense, the setting of Cat's Eye is like any modern city. Modern Toronto, with a population of 620,000, shares in most of the currents of late twentieth-century history. Liberal immigration and asylum policies have brought many refugees from war in the Middle East, which remind the narrator and the reader of the barbarity of Western capitalism, continuing to profit from arms production: 'Killing is endless now, it's an industry, there's money in it' (p. 314). She is also alert to the exploitation of Mexican-Americans (Chicanos) in the California agricultural industry: 'eventually there's nothing you can put into your mouth without tasting the death in it' (p. 403). The fact that it is a grape which produces this reaction suggests a further awareness of John Steinbeck's theme in his Pulitzer-winning novel *The Grapes of Wrath* (1939), which examines rural poverty and exploitation in mid-west America from a populist point-of-view. While neither revolutionary nor Marxist in her outlook, Atwood seems to share in the anti-corporate and anti-imperialist thinking of Noam Chomsky and other North American left-wing intellectuals on contemporary world affairs.

Psychoanalysis

The plot of *Cat's Eye* is largely based on the discoveries of Sigmund Freud (1856–1939), the father of psychoanalysis and one of the most influential modern thinkers. Freud believed that we 'repress' the memory of experiences with which we cannot cope. This repression enables us to avoid unbearable knowledge about ourselves or others but it also causes various kinds of irrational feelings and behaviour called neurosis. He thought that by bringing repressed memories of traumatic experiences back from the unconscious – a term that he invented – a patient can confront and purge them; this was the purpose of psychoanalytic sessions between doctor and patient. The validity of this method of treating mental disorders has often been questioned, but the theories of the conscious and unconscious, repression, the Oedipus complex and the 'Freudian slip' are widely accepted. Freud's book on *The Interpretation of Dreams* (1900) is a modern classic, and many critics have applied his theories to great works of literature. Freud's ideas changed the way we think about the human personality and the human mind. These are now seen as complex entities involving many layers, from the instinctual to the rational, with several components such as the Id, the Ego and the Super-ego operating within the individual personality.

A crucial feature of the psychoanalytical method is the examination of dreams. A psychoanalyst often proceeds by getting the patient to remember his or her dreams, and then analysing them to see what repressed experiences are encoded in them. The result, if successful, brings about the return of the repressed memories, leading the patient to confront whatever it is in the past that is causing the neurotic behaviour. Freud called this process 'abreaction' or catharsis ('purgation', after Aristotle), and several later psychoanalysts, building on his theories, have looked on art and literature as performing a similar office. This is very like the way in which Elaine Risley gradually retrieves her lost years through her painting before the final re-encounter with the cat's eye; it also suggests what she is doing in her narrative, which can be read as a psychoanalytical session. The fact that it is written in the present tense strengthens this impression of a catharsis actually taking place in the course of the narration.

The central character and narrator has dreams in which the terrors of her childhood are encoded as symbols or archetypes, though the author ensures that they can be related to previous experiences by the reader. Elaine's dreams begin when she goes on holiday after her first year of torment. These are nightmares concerning the experience of being buried alive, though this is 'transferred' to her parents (p. 167); the bridge from which she descends to the ravine where she nearly dies; but also objects associated with Cordelia or else with other tyrannical characters such as Miss Lumley and the hateful Mrs Smeath, and other objects associated with her anxieties such as the cat's eye marble, a dead raven, and deadly nightshade. When she reaches puberty she naturally dreams of boys' bodies also. Notably, she never dreams directly of her tormentor although the reader understands that Cordelia is at the root of all of her nightmares (p. 145). This is a classic case of repression.

After she has recovered her memories of the time when Cordelia bullied her so ferociously, Risley still needs to know why it happened. The narrator clearly suggests an answer to this question, though she does not insist upon it very strongly. Freud considered the individual's relationship with his or her father and mother as crucial to the formation of the personality. Cordelia's psychological violence clearly stems from her relationship with a father who appears never to have loved her (pp. 210; 249). Elaine, whose father is a kindly man, receives the emotions of guilt and shame engendered in this relationship at second hand without knowing where they come from. She therefore experiences them as 'her own fault' (pp. 156; 338 and so on) and it is not until the end of the novel that she is able to give them back to Cordelia, from whom they emanated (p. 419) in the beginning. Having reached this point Risley is able to extend forgiveness to Cordelia, and this also brings her own psychological quest to a conclusion.

She forgives Cordelia because she perceives that it is now Cordelia who is in danger of freezing to death if she stays out any longer 'in the wrong time' (p. 419) – that is, stuck in behaviour patterns of the past. Yet Risley gives no indication that she regards Cordelia's relationship with her father as an adequate excuse for what happened. The whole argument of the novel on this score is that we are responsible for our own actions: blame cannot be shunted off onto our parents, our conditioning, our society, or any other villains. Women, for instance, cannot blame the other sex for the way they 'hurt themselves' when they 'fall' upon men (p. 268); feminism based on this kind of accusation is an evasion of responsibility. In these terms, Cordelia's mistake is to accept the judgement of the patriarchal figure: 'when will she learn?', Elaine asks when she observes the dysfunctional relationship in action (p. 249).

Physics

A major strand of ideas in the novel is provided by the theories of modern physics, especially the Uncertainty Principle discovered by Werner Heisenberg in 1921. This principle states that it is impossible to make accurate observations of any atomic particle without altering the behaviour of that particle. It is clearly echoed in the sentence in Chapter 68 of the novel about the way in which the universe has a tendency to change when you look at it 'as if it resists being known' (p. 388). In this respect the behaviour of the universe is like that of the individual personality under psychoanalysis: it shares the tendency to hide its secrets from us.

Heisenberg's principle meant that physicists had to develop new ways of measuring the activity of particles, and this gave rise to quantum physics developed by Max Planck and others. The attempt to unite quantum physics with Einstein's relativity theory led to the unified field theory, sometimes called the 'new cosmology' because it offers a complete description of the universe we live in. Atwood's source for these ideas is Stephen Hawking's *A Brief History of Time: From the Big Bang to Black Holes* (1988), from which one of the epigraphs of the novel is taken. Black holes, however, are never mentioned in the text although they cast a dark shadow over it in the form of the hole dug by Cordelia in which she buries Elaine (p. 107). In this way Atwood dramatises the physicists' black holes as a terrifying psychological experience, making the scientific notion of an indifferent, collapsing universe coincide with individual fear of death and nothingness. When Elaine is covered up with boards and then with shovelfuls of earth, the novel touches on real terror – the kind of terror that has fuelled a thousand 'horror stories' since Edgar Allen Poe wrote about living burial at the conclusion of 'The Fall of the House of Usher' in his *Tales of the Grotesque and Arabesque* (1839).

Though long postulated by mathematicians, black holes were not observed in space until November 1962 when astronomers at the Palomar Observatory in California detected the presence of remote stars called quasars whose gravitational field caused them to collapse in upon themselves. When these 'singularities' occur the volume of a star is squashed into zero space so that its entire mass occupies no space at all, thus creating what is sometimes called 'anti-matter'. Black holes have a mythological status in modern culture, partly enchanting, partly horrific. To some they are big brothers of the 'quark' and 'charm', as recent sub-atomic particles have been playfully called by the physicists who discovered them. For others, they epitomise the processes of a vast universe which is utterly indifferent to human life, and which will eventually collapse inwards destroying everything within it. This event is called the 'crunch singularity' as opposed to the 'big bang' with which the universe is believed to have started.

It did not, however, take black holes to reveal how insignificant human existence can seem in comparison with the sheer scale of the galaxies. Possibly the biggest shock to the geocentric – that is, 'earth-centred' – theory of the universe was the discovery, made by Galileo (1564–1642), that the earth is one of many planets revolving around the sun. With the development of powerful telescopes in the following decades, outer space began to open up and reveal its magnitude to astronomers. The sense of the enormous vistas that then became visible has been recorded by the seventeeth-century mathematician and divine Blaise Pascal (1623-62), who wrote in his *Pensées*: 'The eternal silence of these infinite spaces terrifies me.' The feeling of terror that he felt is a constant background note in *Cat's Eye*, just as the ideas of 'silence' and 'space' are recurrent motifs in it.

Post-modernism

Atwood's narrator character is broadly dismissive of a family of contemporary intellectual movements gathered neatly under the prefix 'post-' – post-structuralism, post-feminism and so on. Post-modernism, the dominant school of thought in this field, is founded on the semiotic discovery by Ferdinand de Saussure (1857-1913) that signs in human language are arbitrary. This suggests that there is no 'truth' in language, only 'structures' which assign functional meanings to their various parts. From this 'structuralist' beginning post-structuralism later sprung, giving rise to a huge array of 'post-modernist' approaches to different subjects, the theoretical groundwork being done by recent thinkers such as Derrida, Deleuze, Baudrillard, Jameson and Lyotard. The central thesis of post-modernism is that everything to do with human culture is 'socially constructed and historically specific', not 'guaranteed' by anything in a higher or transcendent realm (God, Nature, logical necessity and so on). Pushed to its limits, post-modernism asserts that there is actually no 'subject' of experience at all – that is, there is no 'I' or 'you' underneath the social constructs that 'perform' individual behaviour. This view is called, for short-hand, the 'death of the subject', a phrase that follows the curve of 'the death of God'. In addition, such constructs are seen as exercises in power by one grouping or another and it becomes the job of the philosopher to 'deconstruct' them.

Atwood's novel shares many of the features of post-modernist thinking and writing. There is no 'omniscient' narrator (because no one is omniscient), only a first-person monologue. The framework of information in the novel is consciously drawn from a variety of sciences and outlooks, yet none of these are allowed to establish a dominance (or 'hegemony') over the text. Indeed, their shimmering interaction suggests a universe of essentially intangible points of reference, forever 'deconstructing' itself in the light of new trends. Even the Virgin Mary, who probably corresponds to the Protestant longing for a more festive spirituality with a Mother figure in it, is finally denied the status of a 'real' character. Her existence may be imaginary or it may not: at one time the narrator knows she was 'real' (p. 190) at another she thinks not (p. 418). It can only be, therefore, that (as Lafayette once said of love) she is 'a reality in the realm of the imagination'. The novel, therefore, engages with naïve pietism, as in the case of the Virgin Mary, but it does not belong with it: it borrows what it wants from a more 'primitive' culture. This is a quintessentially post-modernist strategy, a strategy called 'simulation' by Jean Baudrillard in a recent book of that name (1984).

Margaret Atwood, however, does make a stand for the subject in this novel. Whether or not the Virgin Mary is 'real', *Cat's Eye* is about the struggle of a highly intelligent and passionately honest character to find out who she is by recovering her lost past in a series of psychoanalytical researches largely conducted through painting. In this way the novel seems to assert that there is indeed a subject of experience, an 'I', if only we can find it. But it does not assert that finding it is easy. It merely says that, in the quest for understanding, there is not much light but there is 'enough to see by' (p. 421). These closing words may be taken as a defence of the embattled liberal-humanist position in the face of attacks from increasingly rampant post-modernism, and a preview of what intellectual life will be like after the post-modernist cult has passed on.

Themes

Abuse

Cat's Eye tells a story about the psychological abuse of a young girl by her school-friends and the effect this has on her personality in later life. Elaine manages to escape from her youthful anxieties when her repressed memories of that time are restored through an encounter with the cat's eye that holds so many painful associations for her. When she has recovered the lost time occupied by those memories, she has still to find out why Cordelia acted as she did: she knows 'what'; now she wants to know 'why' (p. 411), and she wants Cordelia herself to tell her.

Although Risley does not explicitly state the reason why Cordelia behaves so viciously towards her, the narrative clearly shows that the abusive conduct originated in the failure of Cordelia's father to show love for his daughter: nothing she can do will please him; she is simply the wrong person (p. 249). Cordelia passes on her sense of guilt and shame to Elaine, and because Elaine is unable to recognise the source of her tormentor's anger she assumes that it is a punishment for her own inadequacies and failings.

For Elaine Risley the only way to escape from this cycle of neurotic feeling is to confront it at the source in Cordelia's mind. She does this by reconstructing the experiences that damaged her in places where they occurred more than twenty years before. The imaginative process by which she confronts her ghosts in the novel reaches a climax when she finally recognises that the terrible emotions which have always haunted her are not in fact her own but, as they always were, Cordelia's emotions (p. 419). She is then able to forgive her tormentor.

Power

In episode after episode *Cat's Eye* illustrates and explores the nature of personal and social power – the power exercised in families, churches and political states, but also by men and women in relation to each other. Power and its psychological workings are most sharply focused in the relationship between Elaine and Cordelia. When the narrator describes her burial in a deep hole by her friends, she speaks of it as the point at which she 'lost power' (p. 107). In another place she refers to the period of her life when Cordelia had 'such power' (p. 113) over her. The narrative of Elaine's adolescence deals chiefly with the stages by which she eluded that control and established an equal power (p. 233) of her own over the other girl. This begins when she walks away from Cordelia after her near-death in the episode at the ravine in Chapter 35. At this point Elaine detects Cordelia's need (p. 193) to have a victim and learns an ambiguous lesson: 'I see that I don't have to do what she says, and, worse and better, I've never had to do what she says. I can do what I like' (p. 193).

With this she realises for the first time that the girls who have persecuted her are not friends at all. It is her first taste of freedom (p. 193). It is also the defining moment in the novel since it shows that the victim can be equally to blame as the abuser for allowing the abuse to happen (a theory that works better in some real-life cases than in others). Applied to Cordelia, this means that she cannot be exculpated in view of her father's defective love for her (p. 249). What she did to Elaine was her own moral responsibility. As Ben says to Elaine, in a different context: 'You know what you are doing' (p. 85). People are supposed to know what they are doing in *Cat's Eye*, though it is rarely certain that they do: Risley herself is not at all sure when she returns to Toronto for the events of the novel (p. 85).

Elaine's moment of triumph over Cordelia occurs in later years of their girlhood when she frightens her by pretending to be a vampire (p. 233). Some kind of 'energy' passes between them and Elaine is now the stronger (p. 233). This is described as a malevolent little triumph (p. 233); it is not, in fact, a pure victory since Elaine has become more like Cordelia in the process. In a way the two have 'changed places' (p. 227). That is why, as the opening of the exhibition nears, Risley confesses that she is not afraid of meeting Cordelia as much as she fears becoming her (p. 227).

Family

In the nuclear family – called 'nukes' by feminists in the novel (p. 344) – authority ultimately resides in the father-figure: like vampires they come out at night with their 'real, unspeakable power' (p. 164). The idea that a patriarchal figure is behind all power systems is a familiar part of revolutionary ideologies, especially those associated with feminism. According to this view others in society are said to derive their power from him (*patriarch*, 'head a family or clan'), and opposition to the patriarchal structure of society has been a major feature of late twentieth-century politics and culture. In the 1980s subversiveness itself was widely acclaimed as a political virtue: hence the name of the Gallery, 'Sub-Versions', run by women (p. 15). This is a pun on 'version' and 'subversion', suggesting that the works exhibited are 'beneath' the level of official culture and therefore subversive of it (that is, revolutionary).

In Elaine's childhood society may have been patriarchal, yet her own family is an exception since Professor Risley is a liberal who believes that children should be allowed to form their own opinions (p. 96). This is very different from the social and intellectual conformism of the Smeaths. Cordelia's family is, however, nearer to the average family living the 'American dream' in the Canadian suburbs. There are mixed elements of authoritarianism and liberalism in its make-up: Cordelia's father is a charming man, but his authority is absolute and the women in the family worship him (p. 248) But if he is not himself an overt bully, he turns Cordelia into a bully by withholding his affection from her (p. 249). As a result she manifests an extreme form of authoritarianism in the world of children, becoming Elaine's tormentor. A central concern of the novel is to show that children, who look small and cute to grown-ups, are not so to each other: they can be just as cruel (or even crueller) than their adult counterparts (p. 118).

Elaine is so frightened by her experience that she does not want to know anything more about the power in people, though finally she will have to examine Cordelia's reasons for doing what she did. Her own father does not damage her self-esteem, but nevertheless when she is growing up she finds that she does not want to hear about his early life: knowing about people and their inner feelings 'puts you in their power' (p. 217). This is the reaction of an emotionally scarred teenager who is convinced that interpersonal power will always be turned against her. She comes to believe that caring is a weakness (p. 217). Only the journey back to

Toronto that she makes later convinces her that understanding and compassion can be a source of strength.

Religion

The narrator of *Cat's Eye* shows no sign of interest in organised religion, yet the sense of spirituality that lies behind it (and is often occluded by it) is the subject of sympathetic treatment in the novel. Both major Christian denominations, Espiscopalian Protestantism and Catholicism, are looked at. On one hand, Elaine's story illustrates the authoritarianism associated with the Protestant Sunday School culture. On the other hand, Elaine makes Roman Catholicism, with its 'worship' of the Blessed Virgin and its supposedly more sympathetic culture, the object of a romantic fixation. Examples of Catholic culture in its full growth are generally to be found in countries such as Mexico which do not share in the wealth of the industrial West with its reliance on the so-called 'Puritan Ethic'. Such cultures are generally marked by a lack of restraint in iconography, looked down upon by the more 'rational' tradition of Reformed Religion (Protestantism). For this reason, Risley becomes something of a connoisseur of Catholic churches with their 'shameless extravaganza' (p. 197) in matters of decoration. Clearly this shamelessness stands at the opposite pole from the ethos of shame and guilt inculcated by the Protestant evangelists in her experience.

While hardly a question of religious conversion, Risley's shift towards Catholicism establishes a comparison between the warm-hearted religion of Latin culture and the cold-blooded materialism of so-called WASP (White Anglo-Saxon Protestant) society in North America. Elaine's visit to Mexico with her husband Ben, for instance, yields the insight that the people there are still able to move easily across the divide between the spiritual and the material, the living and the dead (p. 387). Their worldview is intact in a way that the emotionally stripped-down culture of the Protestant West is not. The treatment of Catholicism in the novel is less concerned with an act of homage to the older creed than with a mood of disenchantment about the state of industrial society, supposedly based on cultural changes brought about by the Reformation.

The Virgin Mary, epitomising the pietistic traditions of Catholicism, plays a crucial role in Elaine's story since it is she who 'rescues' her when she is freezing to death in the stream at the bottom of the ravine; later it is Mary's words to herself on that occasion that Risley repeats to Cordelia's spirit at the close of the novel (p. 419; cf p. 189). Both of these are emotional transactions rather than objective ones, as she realises on the second occasion (p. 418). There is no suggestion that the Virgin Mary 'really' rescued Elaine; on the contrary. Ultimately the novel encloses spirituality not in a doctrinal but in an imaginative context appropriate to the 'make-believe' of literary fiction. It is presumably in a similar context that she paints a ferocious-looking Virgin Mary with yellow lion's eyes (p. 345) when she starts on the series of pictures based on her repressed memories.

Society

Elaine is first exposed to religious authoritarianism in the Smeath home, where she is made to join in the church-going customs of the family. This causes a silent rift with her own parents who are agnostic (though from a Protestant background). The evangelical ethos nurtured by Mrs Smeath is one of the most painful impressions of Elaine's childhood, mirroring in the larger world the bullying correction of character exercised on her by Cordelia. How the social discipline of the Protestant church works in practice is clearly illustrated in the sections dealing with church-going and Sunday School (see Chapter 18): from the obligatory wearing of hats in church (p. 97) to the weekly memorising of psalms (p. 99), it provides a system of rules governing behaviour and ideas.

That a comparable form of authoritarianism should have been promulgated through the media may seem improbable, yet this was the era when 'responsible' broadcasting and the press co-operated in an attempt to inculcate what North Americans call 'civics' – a cross between etiquette and social discipline. Elaine is bombarded with the fake cheer of the 'Happy Gang' (p. 139) on children's radio. Not surprisingly it fills her with anxiety since she is then ill in bed and deeply depressed as a result of Cordelia's bullying. One of the women's journals from which she collects her scrapbook 'ladies' contains a cartoon impugning trivial misbehaviour in housewives under the intimidating caption. 'This is a Watchbird watching YOU' (pp. 138, 397). This is strongly reminiscent of the notorious slogan 'Big Brother is watching you' in 1984 (1949), George Orwell's novel about totalitarian society of the future.

The way in which Elaine is affected by this two-pronged propaganda is neatly illustrated by the narrator in terms of her shifting attitude towards the stars in the night sky of Northern Canada at which she has often looked with her brother. Accustomed to regard them as remote and indifferent but never threatening (p. 25), she is now taught to think of them as God's spies: 'Now they look watchful' (p. 101). With this alteration in her universe, she leaves the benign world of scientific objectivity inhabited by her father and her brother to enter a dangerous world of interpersonal power. That the torment she imposes on Elaine is a parody of the Christian preoccupation with death and resurrection suggests that Atwood's real target is the ghoulish moral sadism of the Western religious tradition. In this world Cordelia's bullying techniques have free rein.

Gender

The difference between the genders and their roles in society is a central theme of *Cat's Eye* where, as in much contemporary fiction, a map is drawn marking the traditional pathways (dating, marriage), the occasional accidents (jilting, abortion, suicide, divorce) and the common remedies (celibacy, feminist anger, or mature acceptance of differences). Elaine Risley charts her own way in this territory before finally reaching a temperate accommodation of conflicting claims in her marriage to her second husband.

In the childhood sections of the novel her experience of gender distinctions begins on arrival in Toronto when she encounters the words GIRLS and BOYS above separate doors at school (p. 45). After an unsegregated childhood spent playing with her brother, she must now learn how to be a girl amongst other girls without making blunders (p. 47). Later she discovers that boys are her allies against the clannishness of her own sex (p. 163), and later still develops a sense that relationships with men are less hazardous than those with women (p. 378). In fact *Cat's Eye* offers an interpretation of the battle of the sexes which is considerably more hostile to extreme feminism than to men with their residual male chauvinism. Throughout the novel Risley reflects with marked sympathy on the predicament of men in an increasingly feminist age (p. 114), and even seems to wonder if relations between men and women are the worse for men having been shown their feet of clay (p. 267).

When Elaine first experiences attraction towards boys at high school she discovers that the power they have over her is 'held through the eyes' (p. 240). It is, in other words, a given of perception at the moment when she sees them. As a painter she is already beginning to view them with aesthetic impersonality using the trick of looking at their physical shapes without emotional reactions (p. 141) – a trick that she has evidently learned from the cat's eye marble. The virtual immunity to adolescent fever that this confers gives her a freedom in relation to men which distinguishes her from the other girls in the novel. Carol and Susie, by comparison, define themselves in relation to men and modify their behaviour accordingly, while Cordelia tries to capture them as rabbits can be caught in the glare of headlights (p. 243). Later, Elaine perceives that the girls at university who become engaged early on have the look of blind baby kittens but also seem to be full of deceitfulness and greed (p. 276). Such women abuse the power of gender and, presumably, damage themselves in doing so.

Another kind of abuse studied in the novel is the doctrinaire interpretation of gender relations from a feminist standpoint, and it is this distortion that Risley repudiates in her interview with Andrea (pp. 88–91). Contrary to the fashionable dogma, Risley offers the view that there is nothing wrong with women being supported by men considering how much support they give to men in turn (p. 90). The same kind of idealogical distortion is evident in the critics' reading of her *Pressure Cooking* paintings, which they see as stereotypes of women in the role of domestic slaves (p. 151). In fact, as Risley records, the series of canvases in question merely portrays her mother and her cooking methods in various places where they stayed during the late 1940s (p. 151). Both in practice and in theory, then, the relationship between the genders is subject to misrepresentation and abuse. How is such power to be used? And how are abuses of power to be punished?

When Risley joins a feminist group she immediately perceives that the meetings are about anger against men (p. 344). She fails to be convinced that lesbianism is the answer to the problems that arise between men and women, but feels 'ashamed' (p. 378) at her reluctance to get into bed with another woman. She even feels guilty about having so few dogmas (p. 379). As her experience of women's groups increases, however, she becomes more confident in her view of their strengths and weaknesses: their judgements are hard, if fair, and it is easy to appreciate why men are now afraid of them (p. 379). The narrator has earlier observed that, as relations between the genders alter under the impact of feminism, boys not girls tend increasingly to look baffled (p. 114). She distrusts sisterhoods for reasons that we understand from her experiences with Cordelia, and finds it easier to forgive men than women (p. 267). Forgiveness is, indeed, an essential element in the answer proposed in this sophisticated novel, not only to the battle of the sexes but also to the implacable contests of the international world. Elaine's forgiveness of Cordelia in the place where she was tortured by her is an example of this spirit.

Science

Elaine's father possesses a liberal-scientific conception of life, shared in different ways by his children. Elaine ultimately affirms the liberal humanist view of life derived from him, surely the more impressive for being tested in circumstances that cry out for personal vengeance. Stephen inherits a purely scientific outlook in which life on earth is an incidental phenomenon of no importance or duration (p. 217). The setting of his thoughts is an expanding universe full of 'black holes' that will ultimately recollapse and devour everything. He is less concerned about the pending extinction of the human species through its own folly than his father, taking the longer view of the history of time and focusing his mind on the 'big bang' with which it started and the 'big crunch' with which it is likely to end. (See Hawking's chapter on 'The Origin and Fate of the Universe' in *A Brief History of Time*, 1988 (pp. 127–57).)

The difference between the intellectual outlooks of the two siblings can be inferred from the account Stephen gives Elaine of the nature of the universe as the modern physicist sees it. According to him we live in a space–time continuum in which no objects remain separate or unchanged, or remain immune to the fluid process of time (p. 219). Risley's way of organising experience in her art is dominated by this vision of the cosmos as an essentially changeful entity, yet – unlike Stephen – she is not entirely happy with it. What he calls 'space–time' is for her 'the moving edge we live in' (p. 409). For Elaine Einstein's general theory of relativity and its implications define a world that is fringed with anxiety. When Stephen tells her that one twin rocketed away from earth would arrive back younger than the other who remained behind (p. 219), Elaine finds it sad. Characteristically she reads the scientific lore he teaches here in terms of lived experience. Later she will invest his terminology with a tragic human meaning that encompasses the manner of his own death. In this way the Einsteinian parable of the twins returns to haunt her after he has been thrown from the airplane: from then on she will continue to grow older whereas obviously he will not (p. 392). Couched in these ironic terms the narrative of his murder is typical of the way that Risley translates scientific theory into human fact. The novel deals forcefully with the interface between science and humanism in this mordantly intelligent and often witty way.

Stephen himself resolutely remains in the realm of the theoretical and the speculative, showing no capacity for human relationships beyond the casual comradeships of boyhood. He becomes a victim of space travel because – as Risley reflects elsewhere – he underestimates the dangers that surround him in a world of strangers; he thinks it is enough to be who he says he is, but it is not (p. 291). The form of knowledge necessary to 'read' human life is more complex than his equations. The terminology of astrophysics that he uses only takes on full significance when filtered through the punning, open intelligence of his sister with her unscientific liking for disorder. *One Wing*, Risley's commemorative painting for her brother, encapsulates this judgement on the insufficiency of a purely scientific outlook (p. 407).

Time

The first chapter of *Cat's Eye* is exclusively devoted to a statement of the idea of time that dictates the treatment of Elaine Risley's story (p. 3). Behind the view expressed there lies the account of it in Stephen Hawking's bestseller *A Brief History of Time*. Making the point that the laws of science 'do not distinguish between the past and the future'. Hawking considers the possibility that time is no less 'reversible' than direction – North and South, for example. That being the case why can we not 'remember the future' just as we can change directions when we are walking? In the answer that he gives, the 'psychological' arrow of time is shown to travel in the same direction as the 'thermodynamic' arrow of time, which in turn involves the principle that everything in the universe tends towards dissipation of energy and increase of disorder. When the 'cosmological' arrow changes direction so that the universe starts to contract, the conditions will no longer exist for the 'psychological' arrow – that is, for an intelligent species such as mankind (see Hawking, pp. 160–3). Hawking's sentence about remembering the past suggests an absurdity that Atwood has found intriguing enough to install as an epigraph to the novel. It does not, however, embrace a literal question that the reader needs to ask. Instead, it refers to a view of time in which the present is totally implied in the past, so that by extension, the future is totally implied in the present.

Risley's application of this kind of thinking to the personal experiences that she narrates in the novel produces a sense of things less concerned with the physical state of the universe than with what we know about our lives while we are living them. Hers is an autobiographical conception instead of a mathematical and theoretical one. For Risley time consists of layer upon layer of memories, some of them visible and others still hidden in the unconscious (p. 3), but all concerned with the events that make us who we are. Of course this conception is to be found at work in virtually every novel and certainly in every biography. It applies particularly to the formative experiences of childhood which are still *there* in us even if forgotten, shaping our present state of feelings. In *Cat's Eye*, this conception of time actually governs the story, which is about recovered memories, and also the narration, which is conducted through flash-backs. Time, in *Cat's Eye*, is personalised.

Stephen's idea of time is an impassive one: the universe of space–time is expanding and will eventually collapse inward on itself. Time in the novel is not only a 'dimension' but an agency, a force, and not always an agreeable one when reflected in the human body as life gets longer (p. 7). For Elaine during her torment at the hands of Cordelia, time is the relentless measure of endurance. The language of the novel is insistent about its active role in her sufferings: her awful 'time' in the hole is called a 'time marker' (p. 107) separating 'the time before' from 'the time after', and later in life she feels a need to fill in the 'black squares of time' (p. 107) left in her memory by this repressed experience. This emphasis is sustained throughout the novel by an extended series of references to the apparently 'endless time' (p. 113) when Cordelia was bullying her, otherwise called her 'bad time' (pp. 201; 394) by her mother. Time itself features as a malevolent agency in many places: 'Time is passing' and the future is 'taking shape' (p. 139), but she does not want it, developing ways of 'delaying time' (p. 119), and then escaping it by fainting: 'Time has gone on without you' (p. 171). She learns to distrust her growing body because 'time is inside it' (p. 338). For Elaine time seems like a cancer, a disease.

These instances of the term are mixed with other more commonplace uses (such as 'every time', 'the only time', and so on); but as the story moves towards its climax, the idea of 'time' refocuses on the way in which artists confer ' timelessness' on things by making them permanent in their paintings (pp. 151; 409). Risley admits that she tried to confer this time-lessness on her mother in a picture; but it is futile because there is no such thing as timelessness on earth and the pictures, like everything else, are 'drenched in time' (p. 151). Still, as an artist, time is what she deals in, and when she walks amongst her paintings in the gallery, she finds herself later surrounded by 'the time [she's] made . . . which turns back upon itself, like a wave' (p. 409). When she imagines changing places with a bag-lady in the park, she notes that whereas the derelict woman collects shreds of space, as a painter she herself collects shreds of time (p. 386).

Memory

Memory is crucial in Freud's theory of psychoanalysis, and also in the way this story unfolds in flash-backs triggered by the people and places that Risley encounters during her present visit to Toronto. But memory is also central to the plot which narrates the stages by which she recovers the episodes in childhood that have been blocked out in order to shield her from the psychological impact of Cordelia's cruelty to her. For a long time she wilfully avoids remembering these things (p. 303) because of the sense of worthlessness that Cordelia caused her to feel (pp. 199, 372 and so on). Only later when she begins to paint do the objects with which her unhappi-ness is connected begin to emerge in her pictures and her dreams (p. 337). The things she remembers are objects such as the toaster, associated with her childhood masochism (p. 337); she does not yet know where they are coming from, only that they are full of anxiety (p. 337), the chief symptom of neurotic repression.

Repeatedly Elaine is unable to remember the crucial events of her childhood, most particularly her burial and the events in the ravine. Even at the time of narrating, Risley still cannot accurately recall anything about the hole in which she was placed by Cordelia and the others (p. 107). During teenage, she forgets about Mrs Smeath or why she hates her (p. 352); she forgets the stacks of plates, the creek, the Virgin Mary, and all the bad things that happened to her (p. 201). During teenage, when Cordelia reminisces about their childhood together, Elaine suddenly remembers the old bridge but then forgets it just as quickly (p. 232). Later still, when Cordelia accuses her of hating her she finds that she cannot remember ever doing so (p. 359). This kind of amnesia is of course a protective mechanism for Elaine, but it is also a form of death; indeed real death can be regarded as a huge intensification of it – or so Elaine thinks when she revisits the graveyard where the dead people seem to melt like icicles into the river, 'forgetting themselves atom by atom' (p. 418). Forgetting is, of course, as much a part of life as remembering; but because Elaine has experienced such an acute case of it she feels sure she will suffer from one of the diseases that affect memory later on (p. 263).

Justice

'Unfair' is the common childish appeal against injustice. The idea of fairness or justice is one of the points on which Risley's thoughts continually dwell throughout the novel. When Elaine overhears Mrs Smeath talking about her as a pagan after she has achieved so much in Sunday School, the unfairness of it hits her 'like a kick' (p. 179), precipitating the hatred that she feels for the woman. Much later, in assessing her relationship with Mr Hrbik she considers for a moment that she was unfair to him (p. 365); but against this she reflects that young women need unfairness to defend themselves (p. 365). Without it they would be 'in thrall' (p. 365). *Thraldom* is exactly the condition to which Elaine was reduced by Cordelia. The term bears comparison with another like it, 'enchantment', which figures as a kind of misery on page 14.

Cat's Eye makes much use of the biblical saying 'an eye for an eye' with its connotation of vengeful justice. In its Old Testament source (Exodus 21:24) it is used to convey the principle of primitive jurisprudence according to which recompense must be made by inflicting an equal injury on the culprit. In the New Testament, by comparison, Jesus quotes the phrase in order to challenge such a harsh conception of it when he says, 'Ye have heard that it hath been said, "An eye for an eye . . . But I say unto you . . . whoever shall smite thee on thy right cheek, turn to him the other also" ' (Matthew 5.38–9). This is a principle which few people are able to practise. Closer to the accepted ideal is certainly the account of Christian justice in Portia's universally well-known speech:

> The quality of mercy is not strain'd,
> It droppeth as the gentle rain from heaven
> Upon the place beneath: it is twice bless'd;
> It blesseth him that gives and him that takes:
>
> . . .
> And earthly power doth then show likest God's
> When mercy seasons justice.
> (*Merchant of Venice*, Act IV, Scene 1, lines 182 ff)

In *Cat's Eye* the Old Testament formula, 'an eye for an eye', is first encountered as a title for the painting that depicts Mrs Smeath with a half-peeled face (p. 352). Towards the end of the novel Risley reassesses the portrait and its subject in the light of how she herself must have appeared to Mrs Smeath, an unbaptised gypsy from an atheistical family (p. 405). Following this imaginative leap into the mind of the other, the narrator is able to say: 'I have not done (her) justice, or rather mercy. Instead I went for vengeance' (p. 405). By way of conclusion she adds that an eye for an eye only leads to more blindness (p. 405), but elsewhere she suggests a practical reason why we should not be overzealous in demanding our pound of flesh: 'Never pray for justice, because you might get some' (p. 414). All these reflections naturally refer to Cordelia's offence as much as Mrs Smeath's, but also to the offences committed against peoples and races on the international stage.

Terror

Mrs Smeath views Elaine's childhood suffering as a punishment from God (p. 180), and when the Arab hijackers throw Stephen from the airplane, their action is said to be informed by a religious motif in the same way (p. 390). Likewise, when feminists describe men as enemies, Risley detects the exaggerated fervour of religious movements 'in their early, purist stages' (p. 378). In this she follows her father's conviction that religion has been responsible for a lot of bigotry and intolerance (p. 96). *Cat's Eye* has a secular, non-religious, anti-dogmatic outlook; and though it contains many hints that the narrator (even perhaps the author), abhors the workings of Western capitalism, it epitomises liberal values in its assertion of the rights of the individual in the face of every kind of arbitrary 'justice'. In the novel terrorism serves as a marker for the kind of violence that stems from the belief that punishment is mandated by a higher authority of some kind. Those who adopt this view – be they Christian evangelists, feminists, or international terrorists – are suspended between the condition of men as heroes, and men as monsters. Soldiers who die fighting for Islam or for Irish Republicanism are often called 'martyrs', as are other 'freedom-fighters' in many regions of the world. The narrator in *Cat's Eye* sees them rather differently as they put on their pillow-cases and their balaclavas: they are caught between their ordinary selves and their terrifying supernatural identities (p. 390).

It is to the biblical phrase, 'an eye for an eye', that terrorists instinctively turn to vindicate their actions. For this reason the phrase is used in Risley's account of her brother's death: 'He died of an eye for an eye, or someone's idea of it. He died of too much justice' (p. 388). The fact that the saying, 'an eye for an eye' originates in Middle Eastern culture has added poignancy in this context.

That there can be *too much* justice in the world suggests that justice is only itself when it is tempered with mercy, as Portia says in Shakespeare's play. The fact that the play itself is about racial strife between Jews and

Christians, in Venice or in England, helps us to see why *Cat's Eye* should include an episode of international terrorism from the Middle Eastern war of the 1970s and 1980s. In including allusions to such a conflict in the novel, Margaret Atwood seems to make a plea for mercy and forgiveness as the only way out of the cycle of violence caused by implacable ideas of justice as a form of vengeance – a conception all too familiar in Bosnia, Israel, the Basque Country, Northern Ireland and elsewhere in the world today.

Forgiveness

At the outset of the novel it seems that Elaine Risley is seeking retribution; she needs to know that Cordelia has utterly failed in life, or been reduced to the condition of a derelict, or been killed by someone or, even better, survived an attack to live on in an iron lung (p. 7). Yet this is not in fact the way the novel ends, for when Elaine finally reaches the bridge that has played such a central part in her history, she extends to her tormentor the same help that was extended to her by the Virgin Mary: now she can see that it is Cordelia who will perish if she remains stuck in the character shaped by those past events (p. 419). When Risley reaches out towards her in this way, it confirms her own survival as a person while making a declaration of faith in the possibility of forgiveness and redemption in the world and in the illimitably wider universe.

Narration

Style

The style of *Cat's Eye* is almost uniformly that of intelligent familiar speech engaged in telling 'how it was' in the personal past. The register is a witty version of colloquial North American speech with some distinctly Canadian locutions. A wry, ironical tone sustained throughout suggests a private conversation between clever but unpretentious people who share a common experience of the times they live in and a broadly common sense of reality. To all intents and purposes the reader is such a person, and the novel is addressed to us as if the narrator were able to be franker with us than she is with any of the characters in her story, including both her husbands. The conversational style is modified in places by short passages of dialogue and reported speech, but more often the narrative uses a form of indirect speech (*style moyen indirect*) that integrates the thoughts and usages of the narrator's self at previous periods with a commentary added by the narrator in the present. In this way the text involves some shading between language originating with the former and remarks added by the latter. This may require some illustration:

> I know I'll do well in the two Biology exams *I can draw anything . . . I can spell Scrofulariaciae*. But in the middle of the Botany examination it comes to me, like a sudden epileptic fit, that I'm not going to be a biologist, as I have thought, I am going to be a painter. . . . *My life has changed, soundlessly, instantaneously.* I continue my explication of tubers, bulbs, legumes, as if nothing has happened (p. 255; my italics.)

The first italicised phrases are presumably a near-verbatim account of what the high-school girl would have said (or, at least, thought). The second is an evaluation of a moment of epiphany experienced by the adolescent, as viewed now from the standpoint of the narrator, who has become a painter on the strength of it. The phrases in between can be roughly sorted in the same way: 'I am going to be a painter' belongs to the first kind, but 'epileptic fit' belongs to the second. This implies a kind of 'double writing' where phrases can have different meanings according as they are read in the older or the newer context. If two such layers of language merge in a small unit of discourse, the effect can be tremendous. As Elaine eats a turkey wing at the Christmas dinner the narrator says, 'I am eating lost flight' (p. 131). Here it is impossible to distinguish in any final way between the insight of the child and the phraseology of the adult. Both adult and child are, so to speak, co-present at the feast.

In the last analysis, the past and present identities of Elaine Risley are fluid and continuous, and the blending of vantage-points from two distinct periods in the prose of *Cat's Eye* represents the overlap of those 'transparencies' (p. 3) taken from different layers of personal experience which the narrator spoke of in the opening chapter. Because of the distancing effect created by the layers, the tone is generally one of ironic retrospection (though occasionally facetious or sarcastic as when dealing with Miss Lumley or with Susie). What people say – including the narrator's earlier self – tends to be put in brackets for quizzical inspection. At two points, however, this kind of irony is dramatically abandoned, giving way to more passionate outbursts of emotion:

> Damn you, Cordelia! (p. 44)

> Get me out of this, Cordelia, I'm locked in.
> I don't want to be nine years old forever (p. 400).

Technique

Many passages in the novel are examples of 'epiphanies', that is, moments of intense experience or perception presented without authorial comment – an influential method discovered by James Joyce and much practised in his early writings. This kind of writing is set in the present tense because it is the shortest and most accurate way of conveying immediate impressions. The result often resembles prose-poetry, a form of composition practised by many modernists since the nineteenth-century French Symbolist poet Stéphane Malarmé. Among several passages in *Cat's Eye* that call attention to themselves as examples of this kind of writing is, for instance, this description of an approaching attack of illness: 'The air is wavery, filled with light; overfilled; I can hear the pressure of it against my eyes. I feel translucent, like a hand held over a flashlight or the pictures of jellyfish I've seen in magazines, floating in the sea like watery flesh balloons' (p. 136).

The combination of different senses (called synaesthesia) in the phrases about hearing the pressure of the light is obviously caused by Elaine's fever. In other parts of the same episode, the sheer accumulation of domestic detail conveys an atmosphere of great immediacy: 'I lie in bed, propped up on pillows, a glass of water on a chair beside me, listening to the far-away sounds coming from my mother: the eggbeater, the vacuum cleaner, music from the radio, the lakeshore sound of the floor polisher. Winter sunlight slants in through the window, between the half-drawn curtains' (p. 137).

A technique used extensively in early sections of the novel reflects the importance of smell as a form of memory. Risley makes the obvious comment that humans, like dogs, remember through smells (p. 417). A great deal of Elaine's early childhood is recreated in this way. (See, for examples of this, pp. 21, 22–3, 25, 60, 64, 102.)

This technique is probably borrowed from Joyce's novel *A Portrait of the Artist as a Young Man* (1916), where it features prominently in the first chapter. It attests to the fact that we possess a complete system of senses and desires as well as the 'rational' and 'spiritual' faculties that were thought to define humans. In this way, the writing of the novel shares in the enhanced sense of physical and instinctual reality which is one of the legacies of the Freudian revolution.

Vocabulary

Cat's Eye preserves a wide range of terms and phrases from the different decades of the narrator's life as well as others borrowed from the sciences and the arts that provide the referential contexts of her narrative (such as art history, modern physics, psychoanalysis, biological science). Risley habitually collects curious information such as the fact – noted in many dictionaries – that the deadly nightshade is related to the common potato (p. 108). She is also something of a curator of the bric-à-brac of past decades, and many brand-names and names of magazines that were part of common experience in the period of her childhood are included here: for instance, 'LifeSavers', 'Brownie', 'Javex', as well as *Ladies Home Journal* and *Chatelaine, National Geographic, Better Homes and Gardens*, not to mention the eponymous Eaton's catalogue – a Toronto speciality.

Other rich veins of archival material in *Cat's Eye* are the works of contemporary popular songs, and skipping rhymes, including the disturbingly Freudian *'Not last night but the night before'* (p. 140), as well as patriotic and religious hymns promulgated at Sunday School.

Margaret Atwood is acutely aware of the way people speak, of the phrases they use and of the way these phrases have changed in different periods of modern life. This makes the novel a kind of thesaurus of the slang phrases by which people have defined themselves and their world during four decades of the current century. A great deal of this could be put in quotations marks, exhibiting it as language for inspection rather than language at work in ordinary usage. On several occasions Risley invites us to savour those phrases for their amusement value, as when her mother's term for washing up, 'Rattle them up' (p. 29), is held up to attract attention; or when 1960s cant expressions are listed: *'Far out . . . Cosmic. Blew my mind'* (p. 339). Show-stoppers such as her father's now-dated American expletive, 'Son of a gun, son of a gun' (p. 32), get due notice also. More commonly, however, the slang expressions of successive periods are woven into the narrative without comment, though the dead-pan method of delivery often gives them a delightful air of aplomb.

The narrator employs much children's slang and other vulgarities without the least embarrassment: 'farting', 'snot', 'pee' and so forth, are frequent occurrences in the exchanges of the childhood characters while the narrator herself is not averse to saying 'caught some shit' (p. 86) – meaning 'received some criticism'. When, however, Jon's landlord is described as a prick (p. 317) it is clear that this word is taken from Jon's vocabulary though no quotation marks are provided to certify the point. By contrast, Stephen's innocent boyhood way of writing things in urine is an early instance of his disinterest in the less intellectual uses of the body. A more commonplace set of vulgarisms is exemplified by the phrase: *'can I handle the dots?'* (p. 44; my italics) with reference to a polkadot dress that Risley is trying on. This and others like it on almost every page reveal the extent of the author's interest in contemporary colloquialisms that would attract the red pencil in a student's essay. At the other end of the scale, however, the narrator sometimes focuses on words favoured by Elaine such as *besotted*, for foolishly in love, a word that suggests the idea of 'flies drunk on syrup' (p. 285).

A trait that distinguishes the narrator from the author is Elaine Risley's apparent disregard for the exact use of words in several passages: for instance, the phrase 'sopping tears' is used for 'sobbing tears' (p. 172) in one place. It may be true that tears are 'soppy' (a 'sop' is something used to sponge up wetness), but at best this is a popular misunderstanding of the ordinary usage. So, too, is 'dangle' (p. 121) for 'dawdle', meaning to delay wilfully. However, the deliberate tolerance for such errors may be intended as a mark of the fact that Elaine is not a writer but a painter. This is indicated by the fact that her confused sense of the meaning of certain words is at one point said to be the origin of subjects in her painting such as *Falling Women* (p. 268), which is based on the idea of *fallen women*, an outdated expression for 'prostitutes'. Other seeming errors of this kind are 'bi-valvular' for 'bi-cameral' (p. 151), or her description of Stephen's jersey as 'ravelling' (p. 3) in one place and 'unravelled' (p. 216) in another. Atwood has spoken on occasion of the trouble of getting editors *not* to correct her conscious errors. Such errors demonstrate in their small ways that inaccuracy is intrinsic to the processes of the imagination.

Allusions

Cat's Eye is a literary text, and as such it frequently evokes memories of other literary texts (a device called 'intertextuality'). The texts in question, however, are generally those on the curriculum of schools and universities and therefore part of the general cultural equipment of the author and the reader. Shakespeare and the Bible have pride of place, perhaps. Such allusions are intended to evoke their original contexts and the sentiments contained in them. When, for instance, she recalls some verses from Shakespeare's *Macbeth*, 'My way of life/Is fall'n into the sere and yellow leaf' (p. 113), they are those which continue:

> And that which should accompany old age,
> As honour, love, obedience, troops of friends,
> I must not look to have; but, in their stead,
> Curses, not loud but deep . . .
> (Shakespeare, *Macbeth*, Act V, Scene 3, lines 24–7)

Clearly these might apply to Cordelia, whose years of dominating Elaine are recalled immediately after (p. 113). The chain of associations that has brought all of this to mind for Risley starts with the plaid on show in the department store (p. 113). As Cordelia divulges – earlier in real time but at a later point in the novel – 'The Tartans' is the name by which actors refer to *Macbeth* for superstitious reasons (p. 245). Hence the cycle of allusions moves not only outwards towards other texts, but also forwards towards 'unread' parts of the novel.

Atwood occasionally plays games with literary allusions. A lighter Shakespearean reference is found in the name of the Burnham High School that Elaine attends (p. 206), a name perhaps bestowed on it by its pseudo-Scottish principal Mr MacLeod. Evidently he is an enthusiastic admirer of Shakespeare's only Scottish play since Burnham (more exactly, 'Birnam') Wood occurs in the witches' prophecy to *Macbeth* (Act IV, Scene 1, line 91 ff). Although *Macbeth* is a prescribed text for the children's exams anyway, we may be sure that its presentation by the

'Earle Grey Players' (p. 244) is welcomed all the more enthusiastically by Mr MacLeod, since it is the 'Scottish Play'.

Besides 'an eye for an eye' (see under Themes, Justice), the most important biblical allusion in the text is the echo of the foreshadowing of the advent of Jesus in the Gospel of St John: 'and the light shineth in darkness; and the darkness comprehendeth it not' (John 1:5). In its context, this refers to the nature of Jesus as divine Word (Logos), a Greek Platonist conception referring to the order and significance that God imposed on the primal chaos of the universe. In *Cat's Eye*, where the order and significance of the universe is a pervasive issue, this phrase is echoed among the concluding phrases when the 'old light' of stars is seen 'shining out of the midst of nothing' (p. 421). In this way, Elaine Risley experiences an intuition that there is a hope of order and intelligibility for humans in spite of the vast, chaotic processes of expansion and contraction which mark the history of in the universe.

Parody and pastiche

Parody is the imitation of a given style for comic purposes, generally with the intention of showing up what is flawed or ludicrous in it. Pastiche is the practice of making works of art from elements in other works of art, and is not necessarily parodic in intention. The text of the SubVersions catalogue, sampled fairly extensively in two sections of the chapter dealing with the exhibition opening (Chapter 71), offers a glimpse of the contemporary jargon of art criticism – a tendentious form of writing that readily lapses into self-parody. In this interpretation, Risley's *Toaster* and *Wringer* paintings are called 'Early forays ... into the realm of female symbolism and the charismatic nature of domestic objects' (p. 404); her *Picoseconds* is a *'jeu d'esprit ...* which takes on the Group of Seven and reconstructs their vision of landscape in the light of contemporary experiment and postmodern pastiche' (p. 405), while the *Three Muses* picture 'continues her disconcerting deconstruction of perceived gender and its relationship to perceived power, especially in respect to numinous imagery' (p. 406).

It is easy to dismiss these descriptions as intellectual pretension and so they are intended to appear by the narrator. From the standpoint of the reader, however, they offer an added difficulty since, though they fail to describe the paintings in the light of the biographical information that we have about them, they do suggest quite accurately what the novelist is doing in the novel. To take up Charna's second point, the style of *Cat's Eye* is indeed a pastiche of literary and non-literary languages as well as an example of the experimental novel in matters of narration. The paintings too, so far as Risley describes them, can be viewed as post-modernist pastiches of sundry pictorial styles including those of Pieter

Bruegel and Jan Gossaert, to cite two old masters explicitly identified as models in the narrative (pp. 405–6), along with others not mentioned such as American Primitivism and European Surrealism. Risley also insists that the effect of one of her paintings (*Picoseconds*) is to put in question the reality of the figures portrayed in it in view of the manifest artificiality of the composition (p. 406), and this anti-realist strategy is the essence of post-modernism. Even the despised 4-D's diner (p. 363) – short for 'Four Dimensions' – shares in the spirit of the novel in so far as its name alludes to the space–time continuum (that is, breadth, depth, height, plus time) which the novel takes as its formal model (pp. 3; 219). An additional element in the parody of intellectual styles in *Cat's Eye,* is, therefore, a process of self-parody aimed at its own artistic methods.

Humour

Cat's Eye is an amusing novel though its humour is not conveyed in funny episodes so much as in the succession of throwaway witticisms by means of which Risley describes the scene around her. Examples can be found on every page: on pp. 13–14, for instance, we learn that Stephen 'did not exist in the futon dimension', and that Vancouver is as far away as Elaine could get without drowning. The novel also displays pervasively a kind of wit which is not so much downright funny as mordantly amusing, and this is evident in the shape of almost every sentence, as befits the wry manner of conversational narration. In this way, for instance, we find Risley talking about her belief that everyone else her age is an adult whereas she herself is only in disguise (p. 14). The pervasive humour of the prose in *Cat's Eye* draws attention to the nature of the language-making process, its fertility, its variability, its comic and sometimes tragic consequences.

Motifs

Cat's Eye makes much use of recurrent images to build up a picture of Elaine's state of mind as it alters in the course of the narrative. These relate to objects she has met during the period when Cordelia was bullying her. Some are relatively trivial, such as the toaster which she paints in great detail when it rises from her unconscious many years later (p. 337). She knows that such objects are memories though unlike most memories they are detached and clear, having become charged with great psychological significance. In her paintings they serve as archetypes or symbols whose meaning she has yet to interpret when she paints them.

Connected with these are a series of phrases or motifs that occur frequently in the text, serving to chart Elaine's development from episode to episode. Margaret Atwood has taken great pains over the way in which these motifs are arranged in the text, recycling constantly but never disturbing the realism of the plot. Without obtruding upon the reader's attention they establish linkages or echoes with each other (see for instance pp. 104 and 421) giving the sense of something obscure but significant just beneath the surface. In this way the pattern of motifs in the novels represents the feeling of reality.

At times there is a playful element in the way the motifs in *Cat's Eye* are studded in the text. Since, for instance, 'cat's eye' is a dominant motif, all allusions to eyes naturally tend to take on a reflected significance; and hence when the narrator talks about 'eye problems' (p. 5) at an early stage, she is giving early notice of a thematic focus of the novel, although no reader can be expected to notice it on first reading. A little later Risley declares that much depends upon the light (p. 5), an intriguing comment in a novel that begins with remarks on the speed of light and ends with consideration of the light of stars (pp. 3, 421). In context she is merely referring to the signs of facial ageing; yet surely we are justified in believing a central metaphor of the story is being teased out in this passage.

Cat's eye

The dominant motif in the novel is the cat's eye of the title. It is referred to frequently throughout the text and plays a vital part in the development of the story. A 'cat's eye' is the name given to a glass marble with a twist of coloured dye at the centre. This type of marble is Elaine's favourite since it seems to possess the quality of clarity combined with insensitivity to pain that she needs in order to defend herself against Cordelia: it looks like a clear blue frozen eye to her (p. 141). For this reason the marble becomes a talisman that she carries around with her. It is not, however, just a passive possession. It seems to confer on her a secure kind of awareness which she herself had lost, the capacity for immune observation (p. 141).

If the cat's eye has this protective power for Elaine it has another function for the reader. It becomes a symbol for the possibility of seeing things clearly in a world that seems to resist our knowledge, as the psychoanalytical and scientific discourses of the novel repeatedly inform us (p. 388).

References to the cat's eye and its properties are used in the novel to trace Elaine's changing mentality stage by stage as she grows older. When she walks away from Cordelia after the near-fatal accident in the ravine, her state of mind has altered in a crucial way: she feels that there is now something hard and crystalline inside her (p. 193). Sometime before, she has a nightmare in which the cat's eye marble falls from the sky and passes right through her (p. 145). At this stage it has linked up with repressed memories. And when she rediscovers it, finally, in her mother's cellar, it is the crystal marble that triggers off all those memories so that by merely looking at it she can envisage the whole of her forgotten life (p. 398).

Not all associations with the cat's eye are therapeutic. It is closely involved with an insidious image to be met with in the Risley painting called *Deadly Nightshade*. Here the eyes of cats are barely visible in the background (p. 337). Far from beneficent beings, these are the cats whose urine the girls can smell among the weeds where Cordelia finds the nightshade growing (p. 74). Cat's eyes, then, are a two-sided symbol, one side of which is security for Elaine and the other terror. That is why it is such a powerful talisman: it shares qualities with Cordelia herself, whom Elaine recognises as a force of nature in her pure wildness (p. 130). Significantly when Elaine later paints *Our Lady of Perpetual Help*, she gives her the yellow eyes of a lion, making her fierce-looking and alert in the way of a wild animal protecting her young (p. 345). Thus equipped, the Virgin, usually a meek figure, is able to defeat the savagery that Elaine encounters in people like Cordelia. (Elaine herself acquires savagery as a protective cloak during teenage.) The link between the Virgin Mary and the cat's eye is finally embodied in *Unified Field Theory*, a painting that gathers up many of the symbols and motifs used in the novel. Here the Virgin is shown holding an oversized cat's eye marble near her heart (p. 408).

Several other hearts and eyes in the novel relate to this motif. There is, for instance, the bad heart of Mrs Smeath which appears to float in her breast like an 'evil eye' (p. 180). This may be compared with the good heart of the Virgin which also glows outside her body (p. 182), forming a significant opposite to the other. Elsewhere in the novel there are the pickled ox-eye and the turtle's heart in the Zoology Building (pp. 38; 170) the green eye of the radio tuner (p. 56) and the shrivelled eye of the decomposing raven that Elaine finds by the lakeshore (p. 144). Like the cat's eye marble, this eye looks at her but remains insensitive: if you poke it with a stick it will feel nothing (p. 144) – a fact that first puts the idea of suicide in her mind. Through such encounters, the notion of being able to see without emotion becomes the ruling principle of her personality in adolescence. This is a relatively safe position, but it is not particularly human.

Twins

References to twins frequently recur in *Cat's Eye*, serving to establish the existence of a bond between Elaine and Cordelia that lasts long after the period of abuse is over. It is Stephen who introduces this motif when he tells Elaine about the relative ageing of a pair of twins if one is rocketed away from earth and not the other (p. 219). With a characteristic sense of play Margaret Atwood soon adds comical variations in a series of allusion to the twin-beds and twin sets that furnish life among the Campbells (pp. 50–1). Less incidental is the reference to Stephen's briefly cherished love for Bertha Watson which turns him into an identical twin of himself, stupider and more nervous (p. 103). It is, however, the pair of identical human twins greying in formaldehyde in the Zoology Building (p. 169) that imprints itself on Elaine's mind most strongly. Curiously, her encounter with the bottled specimens occurs after the dream in which she imagines her mother having twins, one of whom is grey while the other is mislaid (p. 166), seeming to suggest a premonition – though perhaps it is simply an instance of the author playing with the arrow of time.

As Elaine grows older, she manages to reverse her damaging relationship with Cordelia so that she emerges as stronger. She does this in the graveyard scene where she frightens Cordelia into believing that she (Elaine) is a vampire whose daytime twin Cordelia has known at school (p. 233). In this way, she feels, she has changed places with Cordelia (p. 227), like two 'supposes' (another kind of twins in Shakespeare's *Taming of the Shrew*, Act V, Scene 1, line 120). At the end of the novel, Risley likens herself and Cordelia to the twins who occur as a motif in certain fairytales, each being given half a key to some secret chamber (p. 411). It is only when Elaine can 'give back' to Cordelia her counter-image that either of them can be separate or free.

This twin motif is suggested by *Memory of Fire* (1986), a documentary trilogy by Eduardo Hughes Galeano (*b.* 1940), from which the second epigraph of *Cat's Eye* is taken. The Uruguayan writer reaches back into Indian myths to grasp the psychic origins of contemporary violence in South America. The epigraph (taken from the first volume) illustrates the way in which victor and vanquished are united through the act of killing. In the same way Elaine has taken on some of Cordelia's nature in the course of her triumph over her (p. 233). The notion that the personal power (or 'mana') of the vanquished is acquired by the victor is widespread among primitive peoples, conditioning the practice of cannibalism also. The idea of vampires drinking the blood of healthy young victims is a European variation on this theme.

A further literary model for the twins motif in *Cat's Eye* is provided by the Doppelgänger, a sort of 'split personality' often found in Western fiction: Edgar Allen Poe's 'William Wilson' is a celebrated example and Joseph Conrad's novella 'The Secret Sharer' another, while Bram Stoker's *Dracula* (1897) has also been considered in this light, Count Dracula being an alter-ego of the narrator Jonathan Harker. In such stories, the Doppelgänger travels along with the central figure, emerging to perform acts that express the repressed fears or desires (usually wicked) of the latter.

Bridge

At the start of the novel the narrator describes herself as standing in the middle of a bridge spanning her youth and the years ahead (p. 13). In the ensuing reconstruction of her childhood, the wooden footbridge and the ravine it spans are made the setting of a psychological trauma (pp. 48, 106ff). Later the bridge appears in a dream where she finds herself clinging to its wreckage. Her sense of helpless isolation is symbolised by its being cut off at each end (p. 145). At the height of her period of misery she thinks of jumping off the bridge at the prompting of Cordelia's voice inside her head (p. 155); and it is at the bridge that the Virgin Mary comes to 'rescue' her when she nearly freezes to death (p. 189). When the actual wooden bridge is removed, Elaine has the worrying sensation that someone has been left on the bridge by mistake and remains there though invisible (p. 202) – an obvious marker for her repressed memories. When a brief memory of the bridge comes to mind during high-school days, she quickly represses it again (p. 231).

When Elaine paints her picture of *Women Falling*, it is a bridge they fall from (p. 268). Chief among her latest paintings in the retrospective exhibition is *Unified Field Theory*, and this too depicts the bridge, with the Virgin, the stars, the ravine and what the narrator calls the 'underside' of the earth (p. 408). All of these details are part of a therapeutic review of the psychological trauma she experienced there in girlhood. The final chapter of the novel, simply called 'Bridge', presents a moment of spiritual reconciliation in which Elaine Risley reaches out towards Cordelia with a gesture of tenderness, bridging the gap between them.

Clearly the idea of a bridge plays a vital and polysemous (having many meanings) role in the novel. Nor is the metaphorical sense of 'bridges', so strongly inscribed on Elaine's psychological history, merely confined to the personal aspects of the narrative. It also concerns various dimensions of experience and reflection through which the significance of the novel has been charted: chiefly, past and present, scientific and imaginative, spiritual and material, as well as that of parents and of children, brother and sister, living and dead. Bridging the ravine between these dimensions is a central part of the business of the novel.

Light

Science and religion are conventionally represented as forms of enlightenment. In Christian tradition, for example, Jesus calls himself 'light of the world' (see the Bible, John 8:12), an idea susceptible to many variations. Thus in the hymn that Elaine learns at Sunday School we learn that *'Jesus bids us shine/With a pure clear light ... In this world is darkness'* (pp. 124–5). At Sunday School, also, she is shown a projected transparency of a knight in a forest who gazes upwards at a shaft of light towards which he rides (p. 99), a particularly insipid symbol of the quest for Christian truth in the romantic guise of Parsifal and similar medieval tales. Although Elaine abandons formal religion the metaphor of light lives on in her imagination, as with many other artists.

A no less compelling source of light images in Elaine Risley's imagination is the vision of the reality inculcated by her brother Stephen, who describes a universe of remote stars and echoed light crossing a waste of darkness (p. 104). This causes Elaine to reflect that it seems as if 'everything is made of solid light' (p. 220), and when she first experiences sexual attraction to boys, she feels that they are made of solid light also (p. 240). Later, when she begins to paint, she finds that she is irresistibly drawn to objects made of glass, or those with reflective surfaces (p. 327). The aesthetic ideal that she begins to formulate involves an attempt to depict objects that seem to breathe out light in a kind of 'luminous flatness' (p. 326).

The plot of *Cat's Eye* keeps the motif of light constantly to the fore. It is, of course, implicitly involved with the cat's eye motif and the ideas about sight and seeing generally. The narrator also weaves the light motif into the story of her brother, Stephen. When she finally visits the bridge where she was tortured by Cordelia, one of her consoling thoughts is that Stephen's 'jar of light' (p. 418) is buried under it – an allusion to the marbles he hid there like pirates' treasure. There is an obvious irony in the fact that when he is thrown from an airplane the manner of his death echoes his concerns with the physics of light and Einsteinian relativity: according to his sister, he falls faster than the speed of light to his extinction (p. 391). A ringing note is struck from the light motif in the final sentence of the novel when Risley reflects – echoing Stephen again – that though not much light is visible through the windows of the airplane, yet there is 'enough to see by' (p. 421).

Dark

Risley's preoccupation with light is balanced by a horror of the dark, not in all connections (as when the lights are turned out in a bedroom) but in situations reminiscent of her childhood trauma. All she can remember of the hole in which Cordelia buried her is 'a black square filled with nothing, a square like a door' (p. 107), and whenever the repressed memory of the original trauma threatens to return during adolescence it is as if a 'black door' (p. 116) is opening. The depressions that dog her in adult life as a result of that experience are connected with a sensation of 'black vacancy' (p. 380). Likewise on the occasion when Cordelia starts talking about the holes she used to dig, Elaine's involuntary recollection takes the form of a square of darkness (p. 253).

Elaine's saviour, the Virgin Mary, is represented as a light struggling against darkness: what the young girl sees when she prays to her is a heart with a dark light around it, 'a blackness' (p. 184). When, later in life,

Risley encounters in a Mexican church a statue of 'The Virgin of Lost Things' (p. 198) dressed all in black, she recognises it purely by its colour, which makes it the only one of these 'plaster Virgins' that ever seemed real to her. (What Elaine lost was, of course, her childhood.) The effect of this encounter is to reverse the symbolism, and to annul its depressing influence. It is this meaning which is embodied in the Risley painting called *Unified Field Theory*, where the Virgin appears with a black hood and a black dress with pinpoints of light, her face partly in shadows (p. 408). In this way the Virgin Mary is not simply the negation of darkness but a talisman against darkness which fully recognises the depth and intensity of its power. Only a symbol that does this can be efficacious.

Nothingness

The idea of nothingness (in French *le néant*, in Spanish *nada*), used to express the fearful sense that life is without purpose or significance, is a recurrent motif of modern literature, particularly associated with the writing of Albert Camus and Pablo Neruda. In *Cat's Eye*, Elaine Risley's diminished sense of personal worth, resulting from Cordelia's bullying, is conveyed by means of the same motif. Looking back, she can see that Cordelia made her feel as if she was nothing (p. 199); her recurrent depressions in adult life take the form of 'days of nothing' (p. 114), before which she often senses 'the approach of nothing' (p. 41), and during which she feels nothingness washing over her like a wave (p. 372). At such times she feels inadequate and stupid and thinks she would be better off dead. It is against the background on this insistent darkness of the spirit that we have to measure the temperate optimism of her assertion at the conclusion of the novel, that the light of remote stars provide enough light to see by (p. 421).

Some minor motifs

Several other frequently recurring words in the novel serve to provide pathways between passage and passage, often criss-crossing with each other and featuring in the same contexts. It is difficult to identify these positively as motifs, yet they make a definite impact on the reader as familiarity with the text grows. A good example is the connected words 'edge' and 'cliff', which recur in various contexts while collectively suggesting a kind of risk and vulnerability that the novel postulates as a central part of the human experience, calling for sure-footedness and courage.

Elaine first experiences this kind of anxiety when Cordelia's bullying intensifies, causing her to feel that she is backing towards an edge of a cliff (p. 154). When she finally defies Cordelia she feels as if she is walking over the edge of a cliff in the hope that the air will hold her up (p. 193) –

as it does – and 'emptiness' thereby assumes the role of a recurrent motif throughout the novel (pp. 104–5, 107, 235, 311, 312, 360, 377, 419). 'Edge' becomes, indeed, a metaphor for the psychic environment that human life is lived in: we hear, for example, that young girls 'walk in the dark, along the edge of high cliffs, humming to themselves, think themselves invulnerable' (p. 365). Other 'edges' in the novel connote the sense of remoteness conferred by the Canadian landscape (pp. 25; 41); the tricky 'edge' of fashion (p. 19), and that of time itself (p. 409). In support of this motif, moreover, the narrator expresses interest in the experience of vertigo (fear of heights), or rather the absence of vertigo in Elaine before her period of torment begins. At this stage she is able to sit on the top of uncompleted house-frames without fear of falling (p. 62). Later, when she looks at the pocket of 'empty air' (p. 311) where they watched the Christmas parades from the window-ledge of the Zoology building as children, she experiences a different kind of vertigo related to the experience of time and memory. Also related to this cluster of words and ideas is the use of the word 'vanish', which first describes the years missing from Elaine's memory (p. 108), then the capacity she acquires for making people disappear by dismissing them emotionally (p. 322), and finally the sense that Cordelia will continue to melt into oblivion (p. 413). Behind all of these, the larger and more resonant ideas of presence and absence, memory and forgetfulness, awareness and unconsciousness, being and nothingness, chime in.

Besides these motifs, several other recurrent terms in *Cat's Eye* can be profitably examined, all revealing the care and skill with which Margaret Atwood has composed the novel and the coherence of the themes explored in it. Some examples worth investigating include the following: **betrayal** (pp. 25, 107, 135, 338); **dimensions** (pp. 3, 13, 219, 363 [4-D's], 387); **hatred** (pp. 13, 58, 90, 352, 359); **home** (pp. 49, 129, 164, 189, 300, 329, 377, 419); **silence** (pp. 105, 139, 150, 237, 243, 377, 413, 418), and **wordlessness** (pp. 93, 143).

Part 4

Hints for study

Reading the Text

Cat's Eye is a complex novel and you will need a firm grasp of its form and content to deal confidently with questions on it. After you have read through it once and formed a clear impression of the plot and the way that it is written, consider each of the 'brain-storming' points given below and write short one-sentence answers to them in note-form (not Yes/No). If you are unsure about any one of them, leave it and move on. Keep your notes so that you can expand on them later.

Plot and setting

In what ways is Elaine different from other children? What does Cordelia do to Elaine? What is the effect on Elaine? How does she escape from Cordelia's power? How does Elaine behave towards Cordelia later on? Is childhood bullying the only problem dealt with in the novel? How are gender relationships described? How are the events of Elaine's adult life related to those of her childhood?

What part in the plot is played by a) painting, b) dreaming? Would the story be very different if Elaine were not a painter? What has she gained or lost at the end of the novel? What happens to Cordelia? How do you know?

How much information is conveyed about Toronto? What does the narrator think of the city? Would you describe the novel as a tragedy, a comedy, a satire, a psychological tale, a ghost story, an allegory, a social history, a social commentary, a novel of manners, a novel of ideas?

Character and style

What is Elaine's inner life like as a) a child, b) an adolescent, c) an adult? Why does she offer so little resistance to Cordelia's bullying? Why can her own parents not help her? Is she able to resist bullies as an adult? How does she resist them? What do we know about Cordelia's inner life? Does she develop during the novel? In what way or ways? What is the relationship between the central character and the author?

Why is Mrs Smeath such an important character? How important is Elaine's father in the novel? How important is Stephen? Does he have an inner life? Are there any characters who do not move the plot forward in some way? What is the function of a) Miss Lumley, b) Mrs Finestein,

c) Mr Banerji? Is the treatment of these characters funny, serious, satirical, tragic, and so on?

What style does the narrator use? What relationship to the reader does it imply? Does it illuminate or obscure the essentials of the narrative? Does it sound funny? sad? tragic? ironic? bitter? Is it convincing as a personal way of speaking? What are the advantages or disadvantages of the narrator's style? What sort of vocabulary is used? What would the 'ideal listener' be like?

Structure and narration

Is the story told chronologically? Is there an authorial voice? Is the narrator a writer or a painter? What tense is used and why? What advantages derive from it? Is there any dialogue? If so, how does it differ from other parts of the narration? Are there any passages that express the author's opinion? Are any opinions expressed by the narrator which are definitely not the author's?

Why is the novel divided into titled parts as well as chapters? What is the relationship between the paintings and the titles? Were the paintings thought up by the novelist before the plot or after it? How can we know this? Do the paintings accurately reflect the contents of the narratives? Does the narrative adequately explain the paintings?

Themes and ideas

What is the main theme in the novel? Are there any others? Can they be treated separately? Are they implicit in the plot or are they expressly stated? What conclusions are suggested in the novel? Does the novel make use of any specialised ideas? What context are they taken from? Who introduces them? How are the ideas developed?

What kind of insight (if any) does the novel offer on the views of the world provided by religion, humanism, pacifism, feminism, science, Freudian psychoanalysis, vegetarianism, astro-physics, astrology? Is the narrator for or against Western civilisation, Islamic fundamentalism, environmental science?

Is the narrator interested in the philosophy of time? Is she interested in problems of knowledge? Is she interested in post-modernism? Is the novelist interested in these things? If so, how is that interest expressed? What is the connection between the plot and these ideas? What is the relationship between the narration and these ideas? Do they contribute to the structure of the novel in any way?

Symbols and motifs

Are symbols and motifs used in the novel? What are the most important ones? How are they introduced and how are they used thereafter? Do they have most significance for a) the narrator, b) the author, c) the reader?

What do they seem to mean? Is this a useful way to conduct a narrative? What does it add to a more conventional method? Is there any danger of over-interpreting the symbolism of the novel? Can it be read effectively without thinking about the metaphoric sense of any of the objects named in it? Are objects in novels usually to be treated metaphorically? Are ordinary objects outside of novels usually 'metaphoric'?

Can you make a list of symbols and motifs in the novel? Is it exhaustive or only a sample? How do the following symbols and motifs relate to the plot and to the characters: a) cat's eye; b) darkness; c) bridge; d) silence? Do they refer to anything other than the contents of the novel (for instance the real world, or a higher plane of meaning)?

Which episodes are most dependent on the use of symbols and motifs? How does 'One Wing' function as a symbol in the novel? What does the narrator mean when she calls the stars 'Echoes . . . shining out of the midst of nothing' (p. 421)? What other parts of the novel are brought to mind by this? Is anything outside the novel evoked by this allusion (if it is an allusion)? Do different parts of the novel often refer to each other in this way? What is the general effect of this device on the narration? Is it very noticeable? Is it distracting? Could the story be told just as well without using such motifs?

Critical judgement

Do you like the novel? Why?/Why not? Do you believe the story? Why?/Why not? Which character do you like best? Why? Are the treatment and ideas appropriate to the subject? Why?/Why not? Do you think that it is a good novel? Why?/Why not? Is it comparable to any other novel that you know? In what way or ways? Do you think that it is an important novel? Why?/Why not? Would you read another novel by the same author? Why?/Why not? If you were to write a novel, would you write one like this? If so, in what way?

Close reading

Read the sections on Structure and Characters in these Notes, then read the Detailed summaries. Attempt to do this in one session the first time round (it will take more than one reading to achieve any command of the text even in summary form). In subsequent readings, you should move back and forth between the summaries and the text to check details or reconfirm your own insights. In this way you can develop an impressive familiarity with the novel. The page references supplied in brackets make this easier to do. Be sure to note down striking phrases and short quotations that will be of use to you later.

Now re-read the notes you wrote in answer to the brain-storming questions. Correct them in the light of what you know now about the novel.

Preparing answers

Read through the sections on Contexts, Themes and Motifs in these Notes. Then read through the sample questions given below. Practise writing short answers using the sections indicated to supply points and quotations.

Sample questions

(1) 'We are like twins . . .' (p. 411). Give an account of the relationship between Elaine and Cordelia, with particular regard to the conclusion of the novel.

(2) As a child Elaine was 'rescued' by the Virgin Mary; as an adult she knows there was nothing there, 'only darkness and silence' (p. 418). Describe fully the treatment of this strand in the story.

(3) Discuss the treatment of gender in Margaret Atwood's *Cat's Eye*. Is it a feminist novel?

(4) 'Elaine Risley's loss of childhood memories and her ultimate recovery of them opens the door for a wealth of psychoanalytical materials in the novel.' Discuss.

(5) 'Stephen Risley is primarily a vehicle for a handful of theoretical ideas.' Discuss this statement and give your own estimate of the treatment of this character in the novel.

(6) In what way is the fact that Elaine Risley is a painter significant in the treatment of her character, and how does it affect the structure of the novel?

(7) Give an account of the theme of time in *Cat's Eye*, including reference to its significance for the structure of the novel.

(8) 'An eye for an eye leads to more blindness' (p. 405): write an essay about Margaret Atwood's treatment of the theme of justice in *Cat's Eye*.

(9) 'Autobiographical novel or fictional autobiography?' Discuss the use of the first person narrative in *Cat's Eye* and its implications for the way we read the novel and its meaning.

(10) Discuss the problems you would face in trying to adapt *Cat's Eye* for the radio, the cinema or the stage. What do they tell you about the nature of the novel?

Sample answer

(7) Give an account of the theme of time in *Cat's Eye*, including reference to its significance for the structure of the novel.

Throughout the novel, Elaine Risley is preoccupied with the effects of time, both on her personal life and on the human condition as a whole. The first sections of the novel reveal her anxiety about the ageing process. She looks at older women and herself with a critical eye, and worries about the alterations that time brings to their faces and their bodies. (Later, she looks at her first husband in the same way.) At the end of the novel, however, she is able to celebrate the joy of liberation from responsibility that she witnesses in the friendship of two old women on the flight back to Vancouver. There has obviously been a great change in her attitude in the meantime.

The novel opens with a statement of the theory of time that Risley has developed on the basis of scientific theories told to her by her brother. She knows that time is a dimension, not a line, and she realises from her own experience that past events are still living in the present. In the ensuing narration, she demonstrates what she says here: that our identity is like a series of transparencies in which things that happened long ago are still visible in the shape of our personal present. Even if they are invisible they are still there, since nothing that has happened to us goes away.

Although 'nothing goes away', however, it can be forgotten. The plot of *Cat's Eye* has mostly to do with the way in which Elaine Risley loses her memories of a two-year period of childhood during which she was bullied and abused by her friend Cordelia, who buried her alive at one point and forced her to go down into a frozen stream at another. Cordelia's bullying was essentially psychological, however: she made Elaine feel that there was something wrong with her, that she was 'worth nothing', and it is this feeling that has persisted during most of her lifetime.

Elaine grows up and becomes a painter and then begins to recover images from the lost past through her painting. Later she finds again a glass marble (the 'cat's eye' of the title) to which all the associations of her lost period of childhood had become attached before she put it away with her other childhood things. The memories of the past, which make up much of this narrative, suddenly come back to her. In her subsequent paintings, she produces large works in which she examines what happened, filling her pictures with images and symbols that the reader clearly recognises from the narration.

Elaine Risley's story involves a psychological 'forgetting' that illustrates in a dramatic way how the past impinges on our feelings in the present. Besides narrating this dramatic odyssey into the lost past, however, the narrator deals with human time under a more general form. Risley has returned to Toronto, the city of her childhood, at the time when the novel is narrated, and she goes about her business there in short sections dispersed throughout the retrospective narrative which occupies most of the novel. All around her she sees the changes of twenty years – a time during which the world has entered what is sometimes called the post-modern period. Now our cities and our lives are full of reconstructions of forms and styles that belonged in previous eras. In the design of buildings, restaurants, clothing, we are 'recycling' the past in order to keep up with the 'sawtoothed trend of fashion'.

This is stimulating for those who have not lived through periods being recreated in this way, but for those who have, it is a shock to see the furnishings of the personal past being recycled without any sense of what feelings originally accompanied them. 'The past isn't quaint while you're in it. Only at a safe distance, later, when you can see it as décor, not as the shape your life's been squeezed into.' Risley is angry with the whole tendency of post-modernism, which turns people into 'just a footnote to something earlier that was real enough to have a name of its own'. From the standpoint of the narrator, the idea of time as a series of layers or transparencies is being trivialised in such places as the 4-D's diner, which is a reproduction of Sunnysides, the diner she and Cordelia used to go to, but now it has been 'done over as a museum'.

Cat's Eye opposes this superficial way of exploiting time through its dramatic plot, and also through the way in which Elaine finally extends a gesture of forgiveness and of help to Cordelia so many years after the other girl had injured her. In the world of this novel, people count; the individual has a moral and a psychological existence as apart from the hollow life of mere fashions; time is not just a department store with old appliances 'lining up for re-entry': it is lived existence. Yet it is a perilous existence, since time is exactly the force that is going to obliterate the individual in the long run. It is this paradox that lies at the basis of the value system of the novel.

The idea of time as a series of layers from which the human personality emerges is also inscribed on the structure of the novel, which is presented as a series of flashbacks from the present moment to all the stages of childhood and adolescence through which Elaine Risley grew to be the woman and the painter that she is. From start to finish, the narration is conducted in the present tense no matter what 'time' the events narrated happen in, and this engenders a feeling that time past and time present are somehow simultaneous in the mind and heart of a living human being. The result is an intensely moving narrative which enhances the sense of human worth and holds out the possibility that the experiences of a lifetime can be made to seem meaningful and coherent even as we are threatened with extinction.

Part 5

Suggestions for further reading

Other books by Margaret Atwood

Poetry
Poems, 1965–75, Virago Press, London, 1991.
Poems, 1976–86, Virago Press, London, 1992.

Short fiction
Dancing Girls, Vintage, London, 1996.
Wilderness Tips, Virago Press, London, 1992.

Novels
The Edible Woman, Virago Press, London, 1980.
Surfacing, Virago Press, London, 1979.
Life Before Man, Vintage, London, 1996.
Bodily Harm, Vintage, London, 1996.
The Handmaid's Tale, Virago Press, London, 1987.
Cat's Eye, Virago Press, London, 1990.
The Robber Bride, Virago Press, London, 1994.

Books on Margaret Atwood

DAVIDSON, ARNOLD E. and CATHY N. (EDS): *The Art of Margaret Atwood: Essays in Criticism*, House of Anansi Press, Toronto, 1981.
INGERSOLL, EARL G. (ED.): *Margaret Atwood: Conversations*, Ontario Review Press, Princeton New Jersey, 1990.
McCOMBS, JUDITH (ED.): *Critical Essays on Margaret Atwood*, G. K. Hall & Co. Boston, 1988.
RAO, ELEONORA (ED.): *Strategies for Identity: The Fiction of Margaret Atwood*, Peter Land Publishing, New York, 1994.
ROSENBERG, JEROME H.: *Margaret Atwood*, Twayne, Boston, 1984.
STAELS, HILDA: *Margaret Atwood's Novels: A Study of Narrative Discourse*, Francke Verlag, Tubingen, 1995.
SULLIVAN, ROSEMARY: 'Margaret Atwood', in William Toye (gen. ed.), *The Oxford Companion to Canadian Literature*, Oxford University Press, Oxford, 1983.

YORK, LORRAINE M. (ED.): *Various Atwoods: Essays on the Later Poems, Short Fiction, and Novels,* House of Anansi Press, Toronto, 1995.

Background reading

BELSEY, CATHARINE and MOORE, JANE (EDS): *Feminist Reader: Essays in Gender and the Politics of Literary Criticism,* Macmillan, London, 1989.

FREUD, SIGMUND: *Introductory Lectures on Psychoanalysis,* trans. and ed. James Strachey (Penguin Freud Library, Vol. I), Penguin, Harmondsworth, 1974.

HAWKING, STEPHEN: *A Brief History of Time: From the Big Bang to Black Holes,* Bantam, London, 1988.

LYOTARD, JEAN-FRANCOIS: *What is Postmodernism: The Postmodernism Condition: A Report on Knowledge,* trans. Geoff Bennington and Brian Massumi, Minnesota UP, Minneapolis, 1984.

The author of these notes

Bruce Stewart was born in Ireland where he received his university education at Trinity College, Dublin. He took an MA at the University of California and wrote his Ph D thesis on James Joyce in Dublin. He has taught in the New University of Ulster, at King Saud University in Saudi Arabia, and in the Institute for Higher Technology in Libya. He now lectures at the University of Ulster in Northern Ireland and has served as Assistant Editor of *The Oxford Companion to Irish Literature* (1966). He is Assistant Director of the Coleraine Centre for Irish Literature and Bibliography.